The Crisis for Young People

Andy Green

The Crisis for Young People

Generational Inequalities in Education,
Work, Housing and Welfare

Andy Green
UCL Institute of Education
University College London
London, UK

ISBN 978-3-319-58546-8   ISBN 978-3-319-58547-5   (eBook)
DOI 10.1007/978-3-319-58547-5

Library of Congress Control Number: 2017940204

ALSO BY ANDY GREEN

Handbook of Global Education Policy, 2016 (edited with Karen Mundy, Bob Lingard and Antoni Verger).

Education and State Formation: Europe, East Asia and the USA, extended second edition, 2013.

The Dynamics and Social Consequences of Education Systems, 2013 (edited with Germ Janmaat, Marie Duru-Bellat and Philippe Méhaut).

Regimes of Social Cohesion: Societies and the Crisis of Globalisation, 2011 (with Germ Janmaat).

Education and Development in a Global Era: Strategies for 'Successful' Globalisation, 2007 (with Angela Little, Sangeeta Kamat, Moses Oketch and Edward Vickers).

Education, Equality and Social Cohesion, 2006 (with Germ Janmaat and John Preston).

High Skills: Globalization, Competitiveness and Skills Formation, 2001 (with Phillip Brown and Hugh Lauder).

Convergence and Divergence in European Education and Training Systems, 1999 (with Alison Wolf and Tom Leney).

Where are the Resources for Lifelong Learning? 2000 (with Ann Hodgson and Gareth Williams).

Further Education and Lifelong Learning: Realigning the Sector for the 21st Century, 1999 (edited with Norman Lucas).

Education, Globalization and the Nation State, 1997.

Youth, Education and Work: World Yearbook on Education 1995, 1995 (edited with Lesley Bash).

Education and State Formation. The Rise of Education Systems in England, France and the USA, 1990.

Education Limited: Schooling and Training and the New Right Since 1979 (with CCCS Education Group 11).

PREFACE

This book is about the crisis for young people in contemporary Britain and the politics of intergenerational inequality. It explores the conditions for young adults in the key life domains of education, work, housing and welfare, asking how opportunities have changed between generations, and whether disadvantages faced by today's youth are likely to persist throughout the life time of their generation. Is our society facing the prospect of a genuine generational decline, manifested in multiple spheres, and unprecedented during the last century; if so, what should we be doing about it?

The book grows out of the research conducted since 2013 in the Centre for Learning and Life Chances (LLAKES) at the UCL Institute of Education and, in particular, in the project entitled: *The Crisis for Contemporary Youth: Young People, Opportunities and Civic Values*. This is a mixed-method research project which included quantitative analyses of existing datasets, the conduct of the sixth wave of the Citizenship Education Longitudinal Study (CELS) and also interviews with 100 young people aged 22–26 in 2014. Financial support for this research from the Economic and Social Research Council (ESRC) is gratefully acknowledged (grant reference ES/J019135/1). I would like to thank the current and former research officers at LLAKES who contributed to various aspects of the work, including Nicola Pensiero and Michela Franceschelli contributed to Chap. 2; Golo Henseke contributed to Chap. 3; and Gabriella Melis contributed to Chap. 4. Various more specialist publications from this research will be appearing in their own names in due course.

I dedicate this book to my wife, Ye—a 'pioneer' of the One-Child generation in China and the Millennial generation in the UK.

London, UK   Andy Green

CONTENTS

LIST OF FIGURES

LIST OF TABLES

CHAPTER 1

Introduction: At the Sharp-End of Globalisation and Demographic Change

Much has been written about the changing fortunes of the generations following the baby-boomer generation born between 1945 and 1965. Most in the spotlight have been the Millennials who were born after 1979, grew up during the Thatcher years, and who came to adulthood in the late 2000s, many entering the labour market at the time of the 2008 financial crisis and ensuing recession and austerity. They have been variously labelled the 'lost generation', the 'jilted generation', the 'wasted' generation, 'stagnation generation' and 'generation rent', pointing to their relative disadvantages as a generation born at a bad time.[1] This generation of young people were not only harder hit than other age groups by the Great Recession; they are also experiencing the effects of longer-term structural changes, many of whose origins predated the crisis, and some of which may impact on opportunities well into the future. These include changes in the nature of work, the crises in housing and pensions and, most recently, the ramifications of the UK Brexit referendum vote, which most young people did not support. It is widely held that they face more limited opportunities than their parents and may be the first generation to do so since those born at the start of the last century.[2]

These conditions are often said to be changing the pattern of transitions young people make into adult life. They are living at home with their parents for longer and taking more time to achieve financial independence; they are buying houses later, if at all; and they are taking longer to achieve stable jobs, especially ones which match their qualifications.[3] They are also marrying later and having their first child later,

© The Author(s) 2017
A. Green, *The Crisis for Young People*,
DOI 10.1007/978-3-319-58547-5_1

a trend which some say delays their assumption of adult civic roles and responsibilities.[4] Most of the traditional markers of adult status seem harder to achieve than they were.

The effects of these changes on young people's attitudes and behaviors are also much debated. In the traditional media stereotypes, young people have become increasingly 'disengaged', 'apathetic' and 'cynical.' They show a increasing distrust of politicians and mainstream politics and an aversion to voting in elections which has been rising, albeit unevenly, since the late 1980s. In more complex accounts they are seen as an increasingly isolated generation, who lack the institutional supports of previous generations and feel they must face their difficulties alone. They have a tendency to turn inwards and, as in Jennifer Silva's study of young working-class Americans, often struggle to manage their internal 'mood economy' simply to get by.[5] On another account, they are a generation of pragmatists, who know the generational dice are stacked against them and who are seeking new ways to advance their lives and make their voices heard.

Although much has been written about the conditions of young people today, many questions remain under-explored, particularly those relating to longer-term shifts in the relations between generations. Amongst the most salient of these questions are:

- How far and in what life domains have opportunities for the current generation of youth diminished relative to previous generations? Do the positive generational gains in opportunities in some spheres, like education and lifestyle choices, offset the apparently negative changes in other spheres, like housing and pensions? What is the overall balance sheet of life chances for this generation compared with previous ones?
- Are all young people affected, or is this group of young people so socially differentiated that we cannot speak meaningfully about a generational shift?
- If there has been a major shift affecting young people as a whole, is it one which will impact on the entire life course of this generation (a genuine cohort effect/generational shift)? Or is it more of a temporary dislocation, whereby historical circumstances at a particular time have impacted disproportionately on one age group—those who were coming of age at the time of the financial crisis—thus

delaying their transitions to adult life, but not permanently changing the course of their lives?
- If this *is* a genuine generational shift, affecting opportunities
  throughout the life course, how far into do we see it extending into
  the future? Will this generation be a one-off 'lost generation', disadvantaged throughout their collective life time, but followed by new
  generations which fare better? Or are we facing a succession of generations, each made worse off than the ones preceding by ongoing
  uni-directional changes in economy, society and culture—a scenario
  which reverses the notions of historical progress through successive
  generations to which we have been accustomed for two centuries?
- How would young people and older adults—and indeed the political establishment itself—respond to a 'world in reverse gear' and
  would their responses change the pattern? The electoral dominance
  of the 'grey vote' will continue, but what new political alliances may
  emerge if an unlucky youth cohort carry their disadvantages into
  middle age, sharing common problems with the generation which
  comes after them?

These questions are, of course, hard to answer because they require us to
look into the future. The best we can do is to extrapolate from current
trends, factoring in different contingencies, and remembering that history rarely follows a straight path. Nevertheless, it is notable how little
common ground exists on these issues, either in the research literature or
in public opinion. By no means everyone agrees that young people today
are actually worse off than previous generations of youth, and many of
those who do consider it just a temporary phenomenon. To many social
class differentiation amongst young people renders discussions of generational differences questionable anyway.

To date, systematic analysis of these issues has been quite limited,
despite the plethora of commentary on the current plight of young people. There has also been surprisingly little sustained debate about what
should be done to address generational disadvantages, even in the areas
where these are most apparent. Even within the writings of the most pessimistic 'generational declinists' there is a startling absence of discussion
about actual policies for improving generational equity. We have yet to
see anything like an equal rights movement for young people to match
the campaigns for gender and race equality of the 1960s and 1970s.
Within mainstream politics, governments generally require policy-makers

to assess the impact of new policies on gender and ethnic equality, but no such principle applies for generational equity.

This book focuses on generational changes in opportunities and life chances in the UK, rather than on the attitudes and behaviours of young people themselves. It seeks to advance the debate by exploring the questions above across the key life and policy domains affecting young people's opportunities, including education, work, housing and welfare. The final three chapters propose a range of policies for enhancing intergenerational equity, whilst considering the political conditions which might make such changes possible.

THE DRIVERS OF CHANGES IN OPPORTUNITIES FOR YOUNG PEOPLE

The existing literature provides very different perspectives on how we should interpret the changes in opportunity structures experienced by young people. However, accounts generally agree on the broad social and economic forces, both long-term and more conjunctural, which are behind the what we call the 'crisis for youth.' The main drivers of the changing opportunities have been demographic change, globalisation and the financial crisis and subsequent austerity.

Demographics. Populations are ageing due to greater longevity and a period of declining birth rates between the mid 1960s and 2000s. In the century from 1910/1912 to 2010/2012 life expectancy at birth in England increased for males from 51 to 79 years, and for females from 55 to 83 years.[6] It is expected to rise further by 2032, to 83 years for men and 87 years for women. One projection for 2061 has males living an average 87 years and females 90 years.[7]

While the population in Britain under 44 has remained relatively stable since the 1970s, the older population has increased dramatically, not only from people living longer, but also as the exceptionally large baby-boomer generation is now reaching older age.[8] The two trends are leading to an overall ageing of the population which is likely to reach a new peak around 2030 when the large baby-boomer generation are in their 80s.[9] In 1971 the over 60s represented 20 percent of the population; it is estimated that by 2030 a third of the population will be over 65. The Office for National Statistics (ONS) predict that the number of people over the state pension age (taking account of the gradual raising of this) will increase between 2012 and 2037 by 31 percent, while those of working age will only rise by only 12 percent. Even with later retirement ages, the so-called age-dependency ratio—the number of working age divided by the number of pensioners—will decline from 3.2:1 in 2012 to 2.7:1 in 2037.[10]

Demographic ageing presents a challenge to economic growth generally, as the portion of the population who produce and (traditionally) consume most declines relative to the 'dependent' population of older people and children who produce and consume less in the market but rely more on state welfare services. It also presents a major challenge for intergenerational equity. Welfare states are designed to smooth out risks across the life course.[11] State welfare resources are disproportionately devoted to the young and the old because they need them most. However, the system is based on a social contract which assumes that those who are at prime working age, and contribute most through taxes to the welfare state, will gain their reward when they are old and need to take out more. Over the life course each generation is meant to benefit equally from the ways state resources are distributed. Unfortunately, this system appears to be breaking down.[12] Older people are taking up a growing proportion of state resources in health care and pensions (with the 80 percent of social/benefit spending devoted to pensions and health care—which mostly goes on older people—being the most rapidly increasing area of public spending). The costs are being borne by younger tax payers, with the accumulated shortfall, the growing public debt, passed on to future generations.

Under the traditional intergenerational welfare contract, the tax contributions and welfare receipts of each generation would even out over the life course. But his seems unlikely to happen with the current young generation. They are likely to be paying higher taxes than the previous generation to cover the growing costs of state welfare spending and debt servicing. However, by the time they are old they are unlikely to see the same benefits in pension entitlements (either from state or private pensions) and unlikely to have the same level of health provision. Unlike the previous generation, they will not have the accumulated wealth from housing asset inflation to fall back on if their pensions cannot keep them adequately in old age.

Whether the generational inequalities resulting from demographic change affect future generations of young people depends partly on what happens to demographic change in the future which we cannot know for sure. Some predict that longevity will decline at some point (not least with increasing health problems associated with obesity amongst the younger cohorts). However, the normal assumption is that life expectancy will continue to increase. The secular trend in birth rates seems to be downward, even though some minor bulges in youth birth cohorts may emerge, partly as a result of marginally higher fertility rates from a growing immigrant population (as with those born after 2000 in the UK). However, high age-dependency ratios are likely to continue in developed countries for the foreseeable future. Legislation on later retirement will slightly offset the growth in the net costs to the state of older cohorts, but not enough to restore the previous intergenerational balance in contributions and spending.[13]

What does this mean for intergenerational inequalities going into the future? The disproportionate financial burdens on young and mid-life adults are likely to continue into the future. Future young generations may face the same problems. But there are different perspectives implicit in the accounts that focus on the long-term results of population ageing, and those which focus on specific cohort size effects. A focus on the ongoing process of rising life expectancy and consequent ageing populations suggests that each future generation of youth will be increasingly disadvantaged by the process, in the absence of political action to counteract it. A focus on particular on specific cohorts (and their relative sizes) shifts the perspective somewhat. In David Willetts' account the post-war baby boom-generation was unusually large, and their effects on intergenerational imbalances have been particularly significant.[14] However, subsequent birth cohorts have all been smaller and consequently have less political power. This suggests that the extreme intergenerational imbalances of the present diminish in the future as increasing longevity is offset by the effects of smaller and less powerful cohorts reaching older age.

Globalisation. Globalisation is increasing economic competition amongst states and reducing the capacity of states to raise resources to meet the demand for public services (because of tax competition and the mobile nature of capital). Globalisation seems to be increasing inequality of earnings almost everywhere (although at different rates depending on the political regime in place),[15] through so called skills-biased technological change and declining trade union power, both of which reduce the bargaining power of the low skilled and increase the leverage of the corporations and elites.[16] Globalised capital in a 'financialised' global economy has acquired the power to increase the share of profits going to capital and decrease the share going to wages in many countries (since the 1970s).[17] Global economic competition has also led to major economic restructuring in developed states, with the decline of old industrial sectors and the rise of service industries which become the main source of profit for enterprises. Service industries have generally proved to be slower to improve their productivity than manufacturing industries. One consequence has been that enterprises in the these sectors have been increasingly reliant for their profits not on capital investment and increasing the productivity of labour, but on reducing the costs of labour through various 'efficiency measures.' In a political climate of de-regulation in labour market, this has generally meant increasing the contractual 'flexibility' of labour and reducing the real pay level of the less skilled part of the work force. The has resulted not only in lower real wages for those not in the high skilled jobs, but also in greater casualisation in many jobs. Rates of part-time working, short-term contract working and zero-hour contracts among the adult workforce have all increased in the UK,[18] although perhaps not to the extent predicted in the 'precariat' scenario popularised by Guy Standing.[19] However, the current generation of youth have found themselves at the leading edge of these changes in the labour market,[20] so that they have experienced greater casualisation and a larger increase in unemployment and more wage decline than older age groups.[21] Gaps between age groups in wages have grown alongside a divergence by age in unemployment rates (although these still remain low in the UK relative to many other developed countries). Some predict that these trends towards reduced real pay and casualisation of labour will spread to the highest-skilled jobs as well, but the older baby-boomer generation will have avoided the worst effects of this.[22]

The 2007/2008 financial crisis and the ensuing recession and austerity dramatised the situation of young people because they were the age group which was hardest hit in terms of rising unemployment and declining real wages. But in reality many of the negative trends in youth opportunities started some years earlier, not only in the UK but also in most other European countries. Youth unemployment and the growing proportion of so-called NEETs—young people not in education, employment or training—has been high in many European countries since the 1980s, with the levels of unemployment reached amongst 18–24s in the early to mid 1980s in Britain, during the early years of Thatcher's monetarist experiment, actually exceeding those of the post 2007 crisis. Decline in real wages amongst young people in Britain also

[handwritten margin note: not enough housing in London]

preceded the financial crisis. Most important, the financial crisis was the product of the same longer-term trends which have been impacting directly on young people for over a decade. The increasing financialisation of the economy,[23] and particularly of the property market, which produced the price bubbles and unsustainable levels of lending and debt which detonated the 2007 crisis in the UK, Spain and the USA, has been raising property prices increasingly beyond the reach of young people since the late 1990s. Population ageing has been a marked trend for several decades. The looming crisis in pensions, which will markedly affect the life chances of the current generation of young people as they grow older, was already identified by policy-makers in the 1990s as a likely outcome of population ageing. The economic crisis of 2007/2008 and the following recession, has merely exacerbated these more long-term trends. Young people have been in the front line.

DIFFERENT PERSPECTIVES ON THE CRISIS FOR YOUTH

Most accounts of the crisis of today's youth would broadly agree that the factors above—demographics, globalisation and the recent recession and austerity—are somehow implicated in the changing fortunes of youth. However, they differ in important ways on how these changes are explained and assessed. We can distinguish between four broad types of explanation.

Delayed transitions to adult life. Social psychologists (and others) conduct life course analysis on the basis of longitudinal data on various aspects of the lives of samples from successive cohorts, going back in the UK to those born in 1958 who were 59 in 2017. They are able to show how life course patterns change between generations, how the lives of those now in their 50s were shaped by the circumstances (familial and historical/societal) of their birth and childhood (cohort effects). What they observe in Britain, and in other countries with longitudinal data, is that across successive cohorts, the patterns of youth transitions to adult life have changed significantly. Compared with previous generations, young people today tend to take longer to leave home, gain stable employment, acquire financial independence and to purchase a home. Not unrelated, they are also slower to cohabit or marry, and to start families.[24] Some research also suggests that this slower maturation process also delays traditional patterns of political engagement, and particularly of voting.[25] Life course research frequently identifies long-lasting

cohort effects from the experience during childhood and ι.
years of young adulthood on life chances throughout the h.
However, we will not know for many years from the longitudi.
how the far formative years of the current generation have shaped ι
future lives and the researchers tend not to speculate. They acknow.
edge that there has been a generational change as regards youth transitions, summed up by the notion of 'delayed transitions', but remain
cautious as to whether cohort effects in general will persist through the
life course, thus engendering genuine lifetime generational change in life
chances, and how far this might persist in future generations.

Political economy perspectives on the crisis of youth. Political economists
are generally equally cautious about how far we can talk about wholesale
intergenerational decline. Opportunities in each generation are structured by social class, gender and ethnicity. Class and other divisions are
reproduced in each generation. The political economy literature shows
how inequalities in incomes and have been increasing relentlessly over
time in most developed countries since the 1970s. Countries vary in
their degree of inequality on each dimension, as a result of different institutional traditions and policy preferences, but the trend is in the same
direction in almost all countries.

Rising income inequality is largely attributed to economic globalisation, and the globally dominant neo-liberal policies which have attended
it. Earnings have become more unequal, so it is argued, because of skills-
biased technological change, which puts a premium on higher levels skills
while reducing the labour market value of lower level skills,[26] and because
globalisation has shifted the balance of power further from labour to capital. Power has shifted due to a combination of weaker unions, de-regulation, unrestrained capital movement, and the overwhelming dominance
of mighty multinational corporations.[27] The increasing global integration of markets and the rapidity and ease with which capital, technologies and ideas flow across borders, allows the transnational corporations,
and indeed some smaller enterprises, to rapidly switch different elements
of production between countries, as they search for the most favourable environments in terms of wage costs, access to markets and taxation
regimes. Low skilled workers, and increasingly more skilled workers, in
the most advanced countries, are more and more vulnerable to the threat
of offshoring production to areas where labour is cheaper.[28] This, along
with the decline of trade union power and the increasing de-regulation of

labour markets, gives rise to a continual downward pressure on wages for less skilled work.

Wages at the lower end tend to fall away from the norms in the middle. At the same time, with the spread of complex incentive packages, with payments through obscure share option and bonuses schemes, remuneration amongst the top ten percent, and particularly the top one percent, has been allowed to pull further and further away from median earnings.[29] The wage distribution is stretched at both ends, raising overall levels of wage inequality. Household income inequality increases, not only through the greater differentials in earnings, but also through taxation policies that reduce re-distribution, and through social trends. Growth in so-called 'assortive mating', whereby couples are more frequently formed between people with similar educational and financial resources, also adds to overall inequality between households in disposable income.[30]

Inequality in wealth is generally greater than inequality in incomes and has also been growing. In his analysis of the long-term evolution of capitalism, political economist Thomas Piketty shows that with the post 1970s slowing of growth in populations and GDP in many countries, returns to capital greatly exceed growth in national output, thus raising the ratio of private wealth to national income.[31] As private wealth is more unequally distributed than incomes, its relative growth yields dividends that multiply the effects of the already rising inequality in earnings resulting from weaker trade unions, skills-biased technological change, globalisation and stronger corporate elites. As the ratio of private wealth to national income grows to levels last seen in the Edwardian era in the UK, increasing shares of wealth are inherited rather than earned—already typically over 70 percent in western Europe. This will further reduce social mobility for future generations of young people.[32]

Trends in inequality are subject to policy intervention. As Piketty shows, the substantial reduction in inequalities of wealth and incomes experienced in the years between 1914 and 1970—now reversed—was not just the result of the considerable physical destruction of private wealth during the two world wars, although that may have been a major factor. It was also affected by political decisions to increase public ownership and public spending, which reduced the share of private wealth in the economy, and also by policies on the taxation of wealth, incomes and inheritances, and on minimum wages, explicitly designed to reduce inequality in earnings and household incomes. However, there is also, according to Piketty, a logic in the deep structures of capitalism favouring the long-term concentration of wealth and incomes. If inequalities continue to grow, unrestrained by policy, how does this impact on future generations of young people, and where does it take the generational divide?

Wealth is accumulated through the life course, and older age groups inevitably tend to be wealthier than younger ones, even where most wealth is inherited, as now in England.[33] Wealth is passed on to future generations, and the fortunate amongst younger generations inherit it, reproducing the wealth gaps of the previous generation. As older generations live longer, the privileged amongst the younger generation may have to wait until they are older before they inherit. Others less fortunate may find that their long-living parents have had to spend most of their assets to keep them in old age and have little left to pass on.[34] For the least fortunate, there was nothing for their parents to leave in any case. Overall one would expect that wealth becomes more unequally distributed over time, amongst adults overall, across age groups, and within each age group. At the same time, if the overall mass of private wealth increases, as Piketty argues, newer generations will accumulate more overall over the life course, and so be wealthier on average than their parents. However, an unsustainable public debt could force policy change whereby new generations had to pay off debts incurred by older generations leading to generational declines in wealth.

Incomes are not passed down the generations, or at least not in the direct way that wealth is, except in the case of potential dividends from assets. Over its life course, a given generation will only be poorer than the previous one, in the aggregate, if real terms per capita earnings are declining over the period or if per capita net incomes decline because of higher taxes. At the present uncertain time economists cannot predict with any certainty whether GDP per capita will fall. However, per capita incomes would fall if real earnings per capita stagnated and a greater proportion had to be paid in tax to fund the costs of ageing and to pay off the public debts accumulated by previous generations.

A generational (over the life course) decline in living standards is possible but not widely predicted, even though per capita income in the UK in 2015 was still lower than in 2007. However, as with wealth, we may see a greater inequality within each age group as well as across age groups, in the latter case because population ageing places increasing burdens on young people wherever they are in the wages hierarchy. This does not necessarily equate to the most pessimistic scenario of a wholesale decline in living standards between generations through their whole live course. Nor does it necessarily mean that the gap in earnings of older and younger people will continue to grow, as the generational pessimists tend to assume. But it may nevertheless mean greater disparities and conflicts between age groups alongside the cleavages and conflicts between social classes which run across age groups.

Intergenerational gaps in opportunities and incomes may be largely amongst the least qualified rather than applying to whole generations. Robert Putnam's moving account in *Our Kids*[35] of the changes in opportunities experienced by young people in his generation and the contemporary youth in the USA is essentially a story of growing inequality and how it widens the opportunity gap between poor and rich kids in America. The narrative is framed in generational terms, but the analysis is essentially a traditional social class analysis applied to the younger age group. The prospects for many of the less fortunate children in his survey are shown to be much bleaker than for their parents. But the children from wealthier families were generally not doing badly at all, and certainly not worse than their parents. The account does point to greater inequalities between age groups, but it is far from arguing that throughout its lifetime, the current young generation as a whole will be worse off than its parents had been (except possibly spiritually and in terms of depleted social capital).

The 'lost generation' and the 'one-off' ratchet in intergenerational inequality. This is the perspective popularised in accounts of the 'lost generation' and is proffered by at least one detailed research-based study by former Conservative Minister, David Willetts.[36] This focusses on the differences in opportunities (for work, housing and pensions) of the current generation of young people (born post 1979) and their parents' generation (broadly the baby boomers born 1945–1965). The analysis emphasises the 'unique' characteristics of each generation, in terms of their numerical size, and the particular historical periods during which they were born and lived their adult lives (so looking at both cohort and period effects).

On Willetts' account, the baby boomers were a uniquely fortunate generation. They were born during the years when post-war austerity gave way to increasing economic growth and prosperity but before the major changes in family forms (which to Willetts have had negative effects). They came of age during the 1960s, when jobs were plentiful, unemployment was low and incomes were more equal than at any time before or since.[37] They were the beneficiaries of what many historians now call the 'golden age' of capitalism or, in France, *Les Trent Glorieuses*.[38] Because of the technological innovations of the pre- and post-war period, professional, managerial and technical employment was expanding, providing career pathways for the still small but expanding cohorts of higher and further education graduates. There was more 'room at the top' and the changing shape of the class structure thus allowed increasing social mobility in both absolute and relative terms. The baby-boomer generation (and particularly the males who still formed most of the graduate population) benefitted from rising wages, and subsequently from even more rapidly rising household incomes as female employment increased and dual earning households became the norm. They prospered further on account of other favourable conditions for acquiring wealth. They bought their homes when housing was still affordable and saw their mortgages paid off relatively easily as inflation reduced the real value of their debts in the 1970s. As house prices began to rise rapidly in the 1990s, they often found themselves in middle age with valuable housing assets which they could use as collateral for the increased borrowing which became the basis for their growing consumer spending.

The older baby boomers managed to avoid the worst of the negative effects of globalisation. By the time that major economic restructuring manifested itself in the shake up of working practices from the 1990s, with the job insecurities that attended de-regulation and flexible working, baby boomers were advanced in their careers and well ensconced in their jobs, thus better protected than younger workers. As the boomers reached retirement, many were still able to benefit—just—from generous final salary pensions schemes, and a public health service that was still—more or less—intact. But the post-war cohort not only benefitted from the good timing of their birth. They were also a very large generation, which came to wield great political clout. As they grew older, government policies were increasingly swayed by the strength of the 'grey vote' and favored their age-based interests.

By contrast, according to Willetts, the subsequent generations, and particularly the Millennials, born in the 1980s and 1990s, were uniquely unfortunate, both historically and demographically. They were a much smaller cohort, who would have little electoral power when they came of age. Their transitions to adult life were made more difficult because of the socio-economic changes of the years from the 1990s when the effects of globalisation began to kick in. Those with few qualifications found it harder to get jobs, since the low skilled jobs were being offshored or downgraded in terms of remuneration and job quality. For the growing contingent of graduates, wage returns to qualification began to diminish—or at least to become more polarized and uncertain.[39] Precarious jobs were becoming more prevalent across the board due to the effects of labour market de-regulation but particularly amongst young people, as we will show in Chap. 3.[40] Chances of wealth accumulation were also reduced for this generation (unless they were lucky enough to inherit), partly because rocketing rents made saving difficult, and especially because sky-high house prices made it nearly impossible for most to get or pay a mortgage. These young people were hardest hit of the generations by the financial crisis and ensuing austerity and found it much harder than the boomers to make their way in life. Looking into the future their prospects looked equally bleak. Many would be saddled with much higher personal debt than their parents, due to higher education tuition fees and huge mortgages, and looked forward to paying increasing taxes to pay off the public debt run up by the boomers, and to finance the pensions and health care costs of the growing population of retirees. They would be unlikely to benefit themselves when older from the generous pensions and high levels of spending on health care experienced by their parents.

The lost generation narrative tends to ignore intra-generational inequalities, the differences within generations, but it has certainly brought to public attention to the growing intergenerational inequalities in our society. However, it is principally a contrast between two generations, one which is seen to be uniquely favoured in terms of demographics and historical events, and the other the opposite. Less thought is given to the longer-run structural changes which are occurring and which may shape intergenerational relations permanently. The focus is on relatively short-run historical trends and the effects of successive change in birth cohort sizes. One extrapolation from Willetts' account would be that as the current younger generation carries its disadvantages through to old age, and subsequent generations inherit the new economic and social status quo, lifetime generational gaps will again begin shrink. An awkward transitional era of growing intergenerational inequality will pass, as future generations each experience the same reduced opportunities in terms of secure jobs and house buying and the same diminished safety nets from pensions and public welfare provision. As the larger birth cohorts born post 2000 come to adult life, the disproportionate political power of the grey (baby-boomer) vote will diminish. An intergenerational 'business as usual' returns, as social inequalities, across all age groups, resume their role as the underlying cleavages in society.

A new long-term dynamic of growing intergenerational inequality. This perspective shares much with the account above, with the starting point likewise being the growing gap between the opportunities of the current generation of young people and their parents' generation when they were young. However, the way it analyses the reasons for the growing generational gap is different and points towards a more long-term tendency towards continuing increases in intergenerational inequality over time. In the account by Howker and Malik, co-founders of the campaigning Intergenerational Foundation, a different analysis is provided of the cause of the current divergence in generational fortunes.[41] Howker and Malik are less interested in the size of the different generations and how this may affect political power and policy. They also wish to avoid stigmatizing the baby boomers who they don't see as uniquely selfish or responsible as a generation for the plight of young people today. Their contention rather, is that there has been a radical culture and value shift since the 1980s which is the root cause of the policies which have exacerbated intergenerational divisions. This value shift—which is broadly characterised as increasing individualism—is seen to have its origins in the 1960s, when the young baby boomers were recasting cultural politics, and is thus easily equated with this generation. But it became embedded in the 1980s when the entire political culture was re-caste through the Thatcherite revolution, with its emphasis on rolling back the state, freeing up the market, de-regulation and the weakening of collective organisation (particularly of labour). This went far beyond a generational shift in political and cultural values (with a particular cohort in the vanguard), since it reshaped society as a whole, affecting all age groups more or less equally.

While Willetts maintains that this individualism is primarily associated with the boomer generation who had more 'liberal' attitudes than preceding or succeeding generations, writers such as Georgia Gould dig deeper into the attitudes of today's young, reminding us that they are incontrovertibly 'Thatcher's Children,' formed in the ideological crucible of Conservative and, later, New Labour, neo-liberalism.[42] At the political level, the Malik and Howker account castes neo-liberalism as the main culprit. It has been the policies of neo-liberalism which have been disproportionately disadvantageous to a particular generation of youth because they happened to be in the front line of the changes. However, underlying the new market politics, was a deeper cultural shift to a new individualism that not only sanctified 'free choice' and the satisfaction of immediate individual wants above all, but which portended a new kind a 'presentism' in which the future (and future generations) were subsumed to the needs of immediate consumption and short-term economic growth.[43]

In short, this new culture cared little for investing in the future. Rather, policies were adopted which benefitted the present consumer, property owner and shareholder, whatever the damage to future generations. Howker and Malik note the squandering of the proceeds from North Sea oil; the privatisations which sold off the publically-owned 'family silver' to enrich what turned out to be a rather small group of current shareholders; the selling off of council houses which enriched many of one generation of tenants at the expense of future generation of home-seekers; the Private Finance Initiative (PFI) deals used to shore up the infrastructure (of schools and hospitals) at an inflated cost to be paid by future generations; the post 2008 bail-out of the banks, estimated at £1.16 tn at its peak in 2010,[44] to be paid for by future generations of taxpayers, and the general tendency to acquiesce in—and even encourage—the building up of debts which would literally mortgage the future.

Most importantly, they argue, governments have consistently encouraged the escalation of house prices, not only to ensure the political loyalty of (older) homeowners, but also to maintain economic growth in an economy with flagging demand and poor competitiveness in most sectors baring finance. Recent research shows that almost all of the increased demand which kept the UK economy growing during the 'boom' years of the new Millennium can be accounted for by the growing volume of equity released from mortgages, made possible by the escalating values of homes. This government-engineered hike in property values has led to a wealth transfer of historic proportions from future generations of home buyers to current generation of home owners.

Another worrying manifestation of this extreme 'presentism', noted also by Willetts, is the long-term decline in saving amongst UK families, far in excess of trends in most comparable countries. Between 1990 and 2008 the proportion of household income saved dropped steadily from 3.9 to −4.4 percent in the UK, compared with a drop from 7 to 1.8 percent in the USA; from 12.9 to 11.4 percent in Germany; and a rise from 9.4 to 11.9 percent in France.[45] Howker and Malik say little about climate change but to many—and particularly young people—the failure of the current generation of politicians to deal with global warming represents the most egregious case of sacrificing the future to the present.

What is distinctive about the account here is its deep pessimism. Howker and Malik see the new individualistic presentism not as a pathology of a particular generation but as the new cultural norm. Its implications are deeply depressing because if selling the future for the present is a long term trend, conditions can only get worse for each successive generation, so long as there remains anything left to sell and a sustainable planet to inhabit. They say little about demographic trends but one reading of these supports their case. If the most important demographic forces are not the fluctuations in successive cohort fertility rates, as in Willetts' account, but rather continuing ageing of populations, due to ongoing increases in life expectancy, then widening intergenerational divides can be predicted well into the future.

CHANGING OPPORTUNITIES IN DIFFERENT DOMAINS: EDUCATION; EMPLOYMENT; HOUSING; WEALTH; BENEFITS AND POLITICAL REPRESENTATION

The following chapters provide an overview of changes in opportunities for young people in the key domains which most affect life chances: education, employment, housing, wealth and welfare distribution and political power. As we will see, there are shifting patterns of opportunities in each domain, but each manifests its own dynamic. The evidence for longer-term structural shifts, as opposed to temporary dislocations, is stronger in some areas than others. Where there is evidence of a longer-term structural shifts, what is the nature of the change in intergenerational patterns of inequality? Is the growing gap just between age groups, between the young and older adults, and if so will this persist over time so that future young people remain equally disadvantaged relative to older age groups? Or is there a ongoing cohort effect amongst current young people whereby they carry their disadvantages as young adults through the life course, suggesting a lifetime reduction in opportunities compared with the previous generations? Does this point towards a future where successive generations face poorer life course opportunities than the last?

CHAPTER 2

Education, Education …Under-Employment: The Mantra That Failed

Young people today spend more time in education and gain higher qualifications than their parents did. Twice as many continue in upper secondary education and training and 50 percent more gain degrees than did so the 1980s. Whilst for several decades—from the 1960s to the late 1980s—the UK lagged far behind most OECD states in educational participation after lower secondary school, over the past generation the gap has closed substantially.[1] The UK has now championed 'lifelong learning' and become more like the 'learning society' advocated in so many reports from the OECD and the European Commission in the years after 1980s surge in the global 'knowledge economy'.[2]

This historic rise in participation was encouraged by governments exhorting young people to aim higher in education and by the provision a wider range of education and training opportunities for them to do so. 'Education, Education, Education' was Tony Blair's mantra in Labour's successful 1997 election campaign and a leitmotif of his three governments thereafter. Governments since 2010 had been conveying similar messages. But the rise was equally a consequence of the growing demand for education and qualifications from young people themselves. With the rise of the so-called global 'knowledge economy' since the 1980s,[3] it was becoming increasingly evident that western countries could only hope to maintain their economic competitiveness and living standards in the face of low wage competition in developing countries if they shifted their economies towards the high value-added sectors of production and services.[4] That meant competing through innovation and productivity gains

© The Author(s) 2017
A. Green, *The Crisis for Young People*,
DOI 10.1007/978-3-319-58547-5_2

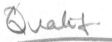

based on high-skilled work. Employers were outsourcing low-skilled work to lower wage countries or keeping the low skill jobs at home at lower wage rates, but demand was high for well qualified school leavers and graduates. For young people born after 1980 the message was clear—if you want a decent job you have to get higher qualifications. Most have responded accordingly and we now have the most qualified generation of young people in history.

But how far does this increasing credentialisation of young people and jobs represent a genuine intergenerational gain in opportunities in—and through—education? Politicians have remained relentlessly upbeat about the benefits of education, and policies to expand education have always been electorally popular. But many academic commentators have been skeptical about benefits of educational expansion. Education researchers, Martin Allen and Patrick Ainley, for instance, have argued that educational expansion has just led to credential inflation for a generation which now has 'education without jobs.'[5] Phillip Brown and co-authors, looking more widely at the changes in global labour markets and the 'global auction of talent', argue that western governments have sold a false promise to workers generally and to young people in particular.[6] They contend that with the exponential increases in the output of graduates from fast developing countries, particularly in East Asia, western economies are unlikely to retain their global economic competitiveness through leading in skills, knowledge and innovation. Much more likely, they say, is that the rising world output of high skills in a globalised labour market, and a trend towards the 'digitalisation' of professional jobs, will lead to diminished opportunities for western graduates and a continuing downward pressure on graduate pay. The era of the high skill/low wage job, they say, is already at hand. The prospectus sold to young people will turn out to be no more than 'broken promises.'

In this chapter we explore these issues of rising qualifications and their implications for life opportunities in more depth, drawing on a range of sources, including the OECD's 2014 Survey and Adult Skills (SAS) and the UK Labour Force Survey. We find that increasing rates of participation in post 16 education and training in England has indeed led to a substantial rise in qualification levels for the current generation of youth compared their parents' generation. More inclusive participation has also narrowed inequalities in qualification outcomes and slightly reduced the social gaps in attainment of qualifications, at least

at the upper secondary level. However, the gains in educational opportunities for young people are to some extent illusory. Improvements in
the skills we can measure, like literacy and numeracy, have not kept pace
with increasing qualifications rates, and inequalities in skills outcomes
have reduced less than those in qualifications, if at all. This suggests that
much of rise in qualifications is indeed a question of credential inflation and yields few benefits to young people today in terms of future life
prospects. Indeed our analysis of the occupational destinations of people qualified at different levels suggests a steady erosion of the value of
qualifications of all levels on the labour market. At the same time career
opportunities for young women have generally improved and, arguably,
for most young people there is a sense that they are freer to aspire then
was the case for their parents.

Increasing Participation in Upper Secondary and Higher Education

Education in England, and the UK more generally, has expanded substantially since the mid 1980s, both at upper secondary and tertiary levels.
Participation in full-time education at 17—the age at which the majority
in England complete upper secondary education—has more than doubled
over the past 30 years, rising from around 27 percent in 1980, when the
Millennials' parents were around the school leaving age, to 67 percent
in 2008, when many of the Millennial generation were leaving school.[7]
On DFE estimates for 2014, only around nine percent of 17 year olds in
England were not participating in some kind of full- or part-time education or training.[8] During the course of 30 years upper secondary education
and training has been transformed from a minority affair to a phase of education experienced by almost everyone, albeit for variable lengths of time.

Increases in tertiary education participation have been almost as
impressive. Of the generation born between 1963 and 1972, who would
have been of tertiary education age in the 1980s, 30 percent achieved
tertiary qualifications. Of the later generation born between 1986–1995,
who were of tertiary education age in the 2000s, 47 percent achieved
tertiary qualifications, an increase of more than half over 20 years.
Participation rates would have been even higher since a small proportion
do not complete.[9] Overall participation rates in tertiary education by 2015
were higher still, nudging New Labour's original target of 50 percent.[10]

Staying on in education and training after lower secondary school has been encouraged since the late 1970s by a number of policy interventions. During the late 1970s and the 1980s a range of new youth training programmes for 16–19 year olds were introduced to deal with the then high rates of school leaver unemployment. The Manpower Services Commission (a government quango) introduced the Youth Opportunities Programme (YOP) in 1978 and replaced this with the more ambitious Youth Training Scheme (YTS) in 1983. These schemes were on a large scale, with the YTS alone recruiting 400,000 16–18 year olds in its first year of operation, representing almost a fifth of the cohort.[11] In 1988 the Government introduced the General Certificate of Secondary Education (GCSE) to replace the formerly divided qualification system—which included 'O' levels and CSEs—with a single integrated examination at the end of lower secondary education. With more assessment by coursework, and lacking the stigma attached to the old CSE exams, the GCSE became popular with students, teachers and parents and is often given the credit for raising the confidence of lower academic attainers and thus encouraging more of these to stay on in education.[12]

Further changes in the qualifications offer came in 1993 with the introduction of General National Vocational Qualifications (GNVQ) at Foundation, Intermediate and Advanced levels, the latter two nominally equivalent to GCSEs and 'A' levels respectively. These were broad vocational courses, organised on a flexible modular basis, with additional core skills, and offering a vocational alternative to the established academic pathway with the potential for progression to higher education. As such they were widely adopted in colleges, which recruited some 250,000 participating students in 1994/5, before they were phased out in 1997 and replaced by new vocational GCSEs and A levels. The Education Maintenance Allowance, introduced by the Labour Government in 2001, provided financial assistance to 16–19 years olds from lower income families to undertake education and training. This probably also contributed to rising participation until it was abolished for most young people in England in 2010.[13] Most recently there has been the raising of the participation age in England which requires school leavers to continue in some form of full- or part- time education or training until their 18th birthday.

Each of these measures has no doubt contributed something towards the large increases in participation seen during the past 30 years. However, the main factor which drove expansion was the increasing demand from parents and students for ever higher levels of qualification in response to the global changes occurring in labour markets. In the 1970s and 1980s early school leavers still had a reasonable chance, at least outside of periods of recession, of securing work in one of the many occupations which did not require qualifications for entry—or at least nothing more than a few O levels. By the 21st century it was clear to young people that there would be very few opportunities available for securing decent jobs if they failed to achieve an upper secondary (Level 3) qualification. With the decline of skilled work in traditional manufacturing sectors, and the downward pressure on wages in unskilled work resulting from global economic competition,[14] the jobs for the less skilled young were hard to find, and if secured tended to be poorly paid, with limited career prospects, and high levels of insecurity. Many of these were part-time, or increasingly on fixed term contracts or contracts without guaranteed weekly hours (Zero hours contracts).[15] Young people wanting decent jobs had little choice but seek better qualifications. That it was demand driving supply and was even more apparent in higher education, where demand for places increased steadily, even in the face of the barriers imposed by new policies on tuition fees. Credentialism came late to England but was clearly here to stay.[16]

Increases in Average Qualification Levels at GCSE, Upper Secondary and Degree Level

The massification of upper secondary and higher education has inevitably increased the qualification levels of young people today compared with those of their parents' generation. Qualification rates have risen at each level of education, as have the highest qualifications held by each successive generation. Figure 2.1 shows the trend in highest qualification levels by different cohorts, using the data for 2011/12 from the OECD's Survey of Adult Skills (sometimes known as PIAAC). Qualifications are classified according to the ISCED—97 classification system,[17] where a Level 5 or above qualification is a bachelor degree or higher, a Level four qualification a sub-degree or technician level qualification, and a full Level 3 qualification is taken to be one achieved through an upper secondary programmes of two or more years.[18] Level 2 qualifications are those pertaining to the completion of lower secondary education.

The proportion gaining a highest qualification at bachelor degree level or above increased the most, rising from 32 percent in the parental

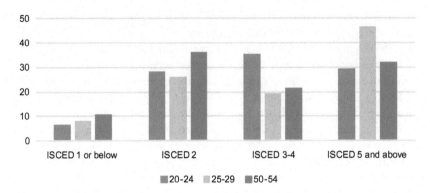

Fig. 2.1   Highest qualifications by age cohort. *Source*: Own derivation from OECD (2013b). *Skills outlook 2013: First results from the Survey of Adult Skill.* OECD, Paris. Data for England and Northern Ireland

generation to about 46 percent in the children's generation (based on the cohort aged 25–29 in 2011/12). The proportion whose highest qualifications were at Level 2 or below reduced from 10 percent in the age 50–54 cohort to around eight percent in the age 25–29 cohort. The proportion gaining a highest qualification at Level 3 or 4 has declined from 21 percent in the 50–54 cohort to 19 percent in the 25–29 cohort, reflecting the growing number of those gaining Level 3 who go on to achieve a higher level qualification. However, the proportion gaining a level three or higher qualification has increased substantially from 53 to 65 percent. Given that some of the highest qualifications held by the 50–54 age group were obtained later in life, and given also that the 25–29 age group would be less qualified than subsequent cohorts, this somewhat understates the difference in attainment rates of those young people going through post-16 education and training in the early 1980s and in the late 2000s.

TRENDS IN LEVELS OF KNOWLEDGE AND SKILL

How far these increases in participation and qualification rates represent genuine improvements in levels of knowledge and skill amongst young people remains a moot point. Many would argue that what we have observed is little more than credential inflation, with much of the gain in qualification rates being attributable to examinations becoming easier.[19] While this may be the case it is almost impossible to verify since the content of examinations has changed over time, along with assessment methodology. Less easily refuted is the claim that levels literacy and numeracy competence have not improved in line with higher qualification rates.

PISA tests of 15 year olds show no overall improvement in numeracy, literacy and science skills in the UK during the 15 years from 2000. In fact there appears to have been a decline during 2000–2006 and little change thereafter. Even if we discount the first two waves, on the basis that skewed samples inflated the mean test scores, there is still no significant improvement over the years from 2006 to 2015. During this period mean scores in England, Scotland and Wales declined in Maths and Science, whilst in Northern Ireland they declined in Science and rose slightly in Maths. Scores in Reading increased marginally in England but declined in Scotland. The changes over time are small in most cases.[20] The general picture is one of flat-lining performance in all these skills domains over the period.

We only have PISA test score data from 2000, and so cannot compare the performance of the today's young people with that of their parents' generation. However, OECD tests of adult literacy in 2011/12 (SAS) do allow some comparison between generations in England. As Figs. 2.2 and 2.3 show, young people in England scored on average relatively poorly compared with those in other countries and, unlike in almost all other countries, mean literacy and numeracy scores for the 16–24 age group were no better than those for the 55–64 year olds.

It can be objected that those in the older age group may have improved their skills during their life course—and there is some evidence for this in England for people in their 20s and 30s[21]—and that they may have been less skilled than the younger age group when they were 16–24. However, a comparison of the average levels of literacy skills of young people SAS, conducted in 2011/12, and in the OECD's predecessor International Adult Literacy Survey (IALS), conducted in the mid 1990s, shows no significant changes over time. The mean test score of 16–24s was 273 in IALS and 265 in SAS. The mean test score of 25–34s were slightly higher, at 277 in IALS and 280 in SAS. But neither change is statistically significant.[22] Furthermore, the analysis conducted by National Foundation

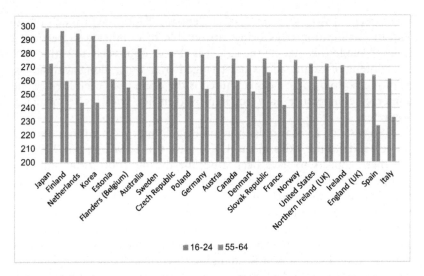

Fig. 2.2   Mean country literacy scores by age group, 16–24 and 55–65. *Source* Green et al. (2014) derived from data in OECD (2013b). *Skills outlook 2013: First results from the Survey of Adult Skill.* OECD, Paris

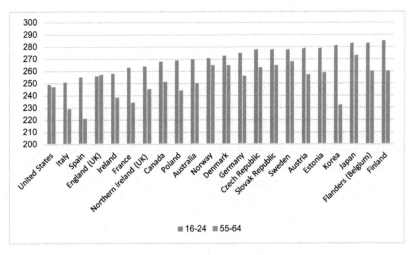

Fig. 2.3   Mean country numeracy scores by age group, 16–24 and 55–64. *Source* Green et al. (2014) derived from data in OECD (2013b). *Skills outlook 2013: First Results from the Survey of Adult Skill.* OECD, Paris

for Education and Research (NFER) for the Government Department of Business, Innovation and Skills (BIS)[23] shows that the mean literacy scores were lower in SAS than in IALS at each education level.

DECLINES IN EDUCATIONAL INEQUALITIES?

Trends in Inequalities of Qualification Levels

A further case that is made for the increase in educational opportunities over time, both in England and in other developed countries, is that inequalities in attainment (qualifications gained) has reduced, both in terms of a narrowing in the distributions (equality of outcomes) and a reduction in the effects of social background on educational attainment (equality of opportunity). The literature on the subject is large and complex, and at times contradictory, and results depend somewhat on the measures used, but the balance of studies show declines in inequality in most developed countries, at least over the decades since the 1950s. Thomas, Wang and Fang (2000), using data on years of schooling for 85 countries from 1960–1990, found a decline for most countries in the Gini measure of inequality in educational outcomes.[24] Meschi and Scervini, using a variety of data sets going back over 70 years, observe a Kuznets type inverted U curve pattern over time with inequalities in educational outcomes tending to rise with initial educational expansion and declining slightly thereafter.[25] In terms of social origins effects on educational outcomes, although some older studies[26] found evidence for a number of countries of persistent inequalities in educational opportunities, more recent studies[27] have pointed towards small declines in social background effects in most countries, particularly at the upper secondary level.

For England, a recent analysis by Sullivan and co-authors,[28] using Youth Cohort Study data for the years between 1990 and 2006, finds declining social gaps in participation at the upper secondary level, as well as reductions in social background effects on attainment. The proportion of places on A and AS level courses going to students from working-class backgrounds increased between 1993 and 2006 from 17 to 20 percent for girls and from 14 to 17 percent for boys. They are not able to provide evidence on social gaps in attainment at A level, but show substantial declines in social background effects on overall GCSE performance, based on a GCSE points score measure and the position of students

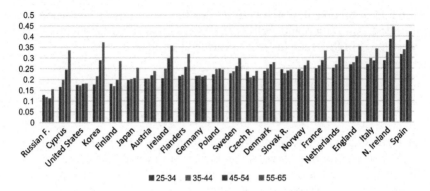

■ 25-34   ■ 35-44   ■ 45-54   ■ 55-65

Fig. 2.4 Inequalities in highest qualifications in different age groups. *Source* Green et al. (2015) derived from data in OECD (2013b). *Skills outlook 2013: First results from the Survey of Adult Skill*. OECD, Paris

from different social backgrounds in the distribution. They find that the chances of working-class boys relative to middle-class boys being in the bottom third of the distribution declined from 2.3 to 1.9 between 1990 and 2003. The odds ratios for working-class girls of being in the bottom third declined from 2.6 to 2.4 over the same period.

Inequalities in educational attainments, at least at the upper secondary level, do seem to have reduced in England over the past 40 years, both in terms of outcomes and opportunities. But the narrowing of the distribution of qualifications across all levels appears to have declined rather less than in many other OECD countries. Comparing across cohorts, using the SAS data, allows proximate comparison of changes in inequalities over time across 24 OECD countries and country regions. Overall inequalities in educational attainment can be measured using education level Gini coefficients for the distribution of highest qualifications (by ISCED levels). As Fig. 2.4 shows[29] there is a marked narrowing in most countries of the distribution of education levels between each of the 10 year cohorts from the 55–65 years olds to 25–34 year olds. Given that the majority of qualification are gained before the age of 25, this suggests a marked reduction in inequality of educational outcomes between the 1970s, when most of the older cohort would have gained their highest qualification, and the 2000s, when the younger cohort would have gained theirs. However, inequality in attainments for the youngest age

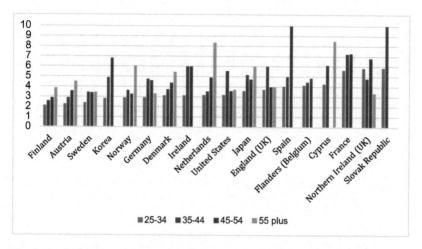

Fig. 2.5 Probability of gaining HE degree of children of graduate parents compared with those of non-graduate parents (odds ratios) by age cohort. *Source* Green et al. (2015) derived from data in OECD (2013b). *Skills outlook 2013: First results from the Survey of Adult Skill.* OECD, Paris

group, and several older age groups, is higher in England than in most other countries and the reduction in inequality across the cohorts is rather less than in a number of countries, including particularly the historically less affluent countries (such as Cyprus, Korea Finland, Ireland, Northern Ireland and Spain) in which educational expansion has probably been more rapid over the period.

We can also use the SAS data to compare the changes across cohorts in inequalities of opportunity at the higher education level. Figure 2.5 gives the odds ratios of gaining a degree between children of graduate parents and children of non-graduate parents for each cohort and across countries. Most countries show very large declines through the cohorts in the relative probabilities of children from more and less educated backgrounds gaining degrees. However, in a few countries, including England, Germany, and the US, the social gaps in higher education attainment change very little between the 55+ cohort and the 25–34 cohort. The pattern in England seems to represent a traditional inverted U curve with inequalities of opportunity rising sharply during the early years of expansion, between the 55–64 cohort (graduating in 1970s) and

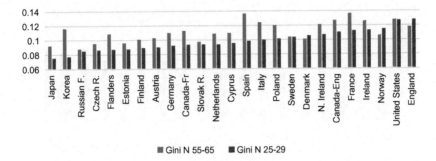

Fig. 2.6 Numeracy ginis for younger and older age groups. *Source* Green et al. (2014) derived from data in OECD (2013b). *Skills outlook 2013: First results from the Survey of Adult Skill.* OECD, Paris

the 35–44 year old cohort (graduating in the 1990s), and then returning to the original level with the 25–34 cohort (graduating in the 2000).

Trends in Skills Inequalities

The expansion in education participation has led to higher average levels of educational attainment and a reduction in inequalities of educational attainment, at least at the upper secondary level. We have seen that the distribution of highest levels of educational qualifications has narrowed and the effects of social background on attainment at GCSE level has reduced over time. However, some of these changes may be due largely to credential inflation. More people get qualifications at any given level because these are easier to get than they used to be. Because attainment at each level is more inclusive, there appears to have been a significant decline in inequalities in educational attainment below degree level. If we look at the trends in skills inequalities we may get a somewhat different picture of what has happened.

The SAS data show that skills distributions for England in both literacy and numeracy were wider amongst 25–29 year olds than amongst 55–65 year olds (See Fig. 2.6 for numeracy), but this may be explained partly by a narrowing in skills distributions during the middle years of the life course in countries with exceptionally unequal skills.[30] The best evidence we have on the trends in skills distribution amongst young

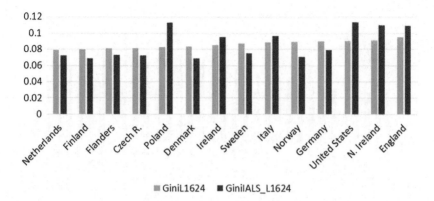

Fig. 2.7 Literacy ginis for 16–24 year olds in IALS and SAS. *Source* Green et al. (2014) derived from data in OECD (2013b). *Skills outlook* 2013: *First results from the Survey of Adult Skill.* OECD, Paris

people is from a comparison between skills distribution for literacy in IALS, conducted in 1996 and in SAS, conducted in 2011/12. What this shows is a very slight narrowing of the distribution for 16–24s in England during the period from 1996 to 2011. However, literacy skills in England were still more widely distributed than in any of the other OECD countries in both IALS and SAS surveys (Fig. 2.7).

The trend in social background effects on skills, however, is much more negative in England. The SAS data show that inequality of opportunities in numeracy and literacy skills is much higher amongst young people (aged 16–24s) than older people (aged 55–65).[31] Again some of this difference may be due to a decline in the social gaps in skills over the life course which we are unable to verify. But this seems unlikely to account for an increase in the social gap in scores in numeracy of the magnitude we see for England. Here the difference between the mean scores of respondents with graduate parents and those with non-gradate parents increases by 28 points, from 39 points in the 55 + generation to 67 points in the 16–24 generation (See Fig. 2.8). Across OECD countries, an additional 28 points is equivalent, on average, to four years of schooling.[32] Inequality is also much higher on average in England and other English-speaking countries than in Nordic, Southern European and East Asian countries.

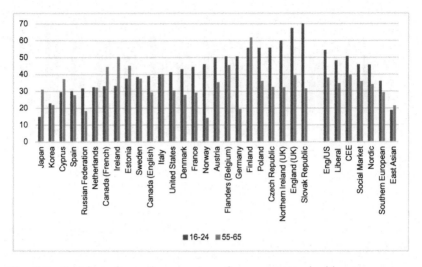

Fig. 2.8 Social gradients for numeracy for younger and older age groups. *Source* Green et al. (2014) derived from data in OECD (2013b). *Skills outlook 2013: First results from the Survey of Adult Skill.* OECD, Paris

EXPLAINING THE TRENDS IN SKILLS INEQUALITIES

The evidence on trends in skills inequalities in England presents a much less sanguine picture of declining inequalities than we get from looking at qualification levels. Whilst the latter suggests a significant reduction in inequalities of opportunities and outcomes, particularly at the upper secondary level, the skills evidence suggests that inequality of opportunity in skills has risen substantially, even if there has been a slight narrowing in the skills distribution for young people over time. In many ways this conforms better to the dominant theories that seek to explain trends in educational inequalities.

According to Raymond Boudon's influential 'positional' theory, social inequalities in education are reproduced in two ways which he refers to as the primary and secondary effects of social stratification.[33] Primary effects occur as a result of the transmission of cultural capital within the family, so that children who experience high levels of cultural capital at home achieve better in schools that value the same forms of cultural capital. Secondary effects occur as a result of children from different backgrounds making different choices within the education system, whereby children from higher status families, for instance, are more likely to choose pathways that lead to higher status qualifications, even when they are the same level of tested achievement. The first process tends to occur, arguably, in a similar way in all societies and education systems.[34] However, the second process may be more conditional on the nature of the particular education system. As Boudon cogently argued, in societies structured by class and other inequalities, the greater the variety of different routes through the education system—i.e. the more 'branching-off' points—the greater the likelihood that socially differentiated aspirations and expectations, engendered from outside the education system, will structure student choices, even in a situation of ostensibly meritocratic access, so that educational opportunities and outcomes will be structured along class, race and gender lines.

In more recently elaborated theories of 'persistent inequalities' in education, elite social groups maintain their educational advantages as education systems expand in two ways. According to the theory of Maximally Maintained Inequality (MMI),[35] as a phase of the education systems expands, higher social groups can maintain their advantage so long as their participation in that phase of education grows as fast as, or faster than that of lower social groups. However, when participation by elite students reaches saturation levels, participation rates for children from lower social groups catch up, thus equalising opportunities at that level. Positional competition by social groups then tends to shift to higher levels of education. At the same time, according to the Effectively Maintained Inequality (EMI) theory,[36] mass provision at the lower level develops more differentiated pathways, increasingly organised into a status hierarchy, with elite students tending to colonise the most prestigious tracks with the best progression routes to higher levels of education.

Both of these processes can be identified in the evolution of further and higher education in England. As rises in participation in further education since the 1980s led to near universal participation by the 2000s, social gaps in participation have declined and positional competition has focussed increasingly on higher education, thus driving rising enrolments there. The equalisation of participation in upper secondary education and training has reduced inequalities in educational qualifications at that level, while elites have maintained their advantages at the higher education level. This has most likely been achieved through the processes described in EMI theory whereby as each level has expanded it has become increasingly differentiated into multiple pathways defined in a status hierarchy, with elite groups dominating the highest status pathways that provide access to the best opportunities at the higher level. The process has been very evident in the development of upper secondary education and training in England over the past 40 years.

During the 1970s, when barely a third of young people stayed on in education and training after 15/16, there were just two main pathways. One was the A level studies in the Sixth Form or Sixth Form College which constituted the 'royal road' to higher education. The other was the vocational route, consisting then mainly of craft apprenticeships which, before their decline in the mid 1970s, enrolled up to a third of working-class boys, but very few girls. Both pathways had relatively clear progression routes and predictable future opportunities in the labour market. With the expansion of participation since the late 1970s there has been a proliferation of new programmes and qualifications of very unequal duration and status and with very different prospects in terms of progression to higher levels education and training or into the labour market. A similar diversification of pathways has been observed at the higher education level, not only with the status distinctions between institutions—such as between those belonging, respectively, to the Russel Group, the 94 Group, and the Local Million Plus Group—but also between students studying full- and part-time, and those studying at the local institution and those going away from home to university.[37] In the face of the great diversity of qualifications, national qualification frameworks have been adopted to establish equivalences between academic and vocational qualifications at different levels, and university first degrees are all theoretically equivalent. This has contributed towards an apparent equalisation of attainment at different levels. However, it disguises the fact that in terms of measured skills inequality persists to much the same degree as before.

Recent comparative research, using quasi cohorts drawn from the PISA and SAS surveys, estimates the life course changes in skills inequalities between the ages of 15 and 27, and suggests that upper secondary education and training mitigates skills inequality much less in England than in most other OECD countries which participated in both surveys.[38] Numeracy skills inequality actually increased substantially in England during this phase of education. The research also shows that relative failure in reducing skills inequality is associated across countries with systems which have a proliferation of different types of programme, of varying quality and duration, and which do not have a mandatory common core of learning in maths and the national language. All of this casts doubt on how far educational opportunities for the current generation of youth are actually better than they were for their parents, 30 years before. In the following section, we examine the anatomy of the different pathways as they exist today.

PATHWAYS IN POST 16 EDUCATION AND TRAINING

Upper secondary education in England has traditionally been understood to start at 16, after most students have complete their GCSEs (or previously 0 levels) and when they move into the Sixth Form or transfer to a Sixth Form College, or Further Education College. There are currently over three thousand different qualifications which can be taken during this phase,[39] and different modes of studying each, but we can broadly distinguish between four main pathways corresponding to different levels of qualification. Annual data from the DFE (2015) gives the best estimates of the proportion of each age group studying at each level. The median age of students leaving upper secondary education and training is 17, so it is best to use this age group to identify the proportions following each pathway (even though some may have been in different pathways at 16). Two pathways constitute what may be called 'full' upper secondary education and training—that is the one that meets the OECD's criteria for ISCED Level 3 (long).

The 'royal road' remains the A level academic pathway which included 43 percent of 17 year olds in 2014, enrolled, normally full-time, either in sixth forms, Sixth Form Colleges or FE Colleges. Compared with other pathways this one has the clearest identity and is still the best known to the public and politicians. A levels are still considered the 'gold standard'. Those of our interviewees who had followed this route, tended to describe relatively smooth transitions from lower secondary education into upper secondary with progression paths thereafter as fairly linear and predictable. They had quite clear goals, generally supported by high parental aspirations, and planned their routes towards achieving these goals. They were able to recall the successive steps in their educational journeys with ease, noting the names of the courses they followed and the grades they achieved. Overall, they possessed relatively strong identities as students following an established and respected path, whose outcome was more or less predictable providing they worked hard.

In addition to the A level route—or sometimes combined with it—is the Level 3 vocational pathway which enrolled about 21 percent of 17 year olds in 2014. This pathway consists mainly of students studying full-time in sixth forms or colleges for long-standing vocational qualifications, such as the BTEC National Diploma, or on courses leading to the recently re-styled Applied General or more vocationally-specific Tech Level awards. It also includes a small proportion of apprentices and trainees taking Level 3 NVQs who enrolled in programmes organised by employers and private training organisations. Graduates from this pathway will either progress into higher education or go directly into the labour market. We may call this the 'higher vocational pathway.' This type of upper secondary education and training lacks the clear identity of the A level route, not least because it includes such a plethora of qualifications and different ways of studying. Nevertheless, its more prestigious qualifications, such as the BTEC National Diploma, and some Level 3 NVQs, such as City and Guilds qualifications, are well known and students generally have a clear vocational orientation. Some 25 percent of those gaining these qualifications make it into higher education.[40]

Taken together, these two pathways account for the two thirds of young people, most of whom achieve qualifications which will allow progression to further study or career path jobs.

There remains a third of young people who take other pathways which do not generally lead to Level 3 qualifications and which offer much poorer prospects of progression into further education or career path jobs. These include around 8.1 percent of 17 year olds who are taking Level 2 academic qualifications, such as GCSEs, or vocational qualifications such as BTEC Intermediates, now often re-styled as Tech certificates, who are mostly enrolled full- or part-time in colleges. Their courses are normally designed to last for one year or less, but many remain on such courses for several years.[41] A further 4.1 percent were taking courses leading only to Level 1 qualifications. In addition to this 6.9 percent are classified as being in 'work-based learning', who are mostly on Level 2 Apprenticeship programmes, and 7.5 percent in other private training. The majority of these two groups will not get qualifications above Level 2.[42] In addition to those above in education or training there were 5.4 percent of 17 year olds not in education, employment or training (NEET) and 3.6 percent who were employed but receiving no training. This latter group tends to move in an out of education and so cannot really be considered to constitute a discrete pathway.

Together these two routes represent the least prestigious pathway through 16–19 education and training, including many of the most vulnerable students. Our interviewees who had taken this route tended to come from poorer families with more disrupted home lives and less parental support. Their goals were often not very clear and they often switched between different courses, or from a course to a job and then back to college, or in and out of education and NEETdom. Many courses were left unfinished and qualifications abandoned. What was most striking in young people's accounts of their studies was the sheer lack of identity and purposefulness of their studies. Most could not give the actual name of the qualification they were taking and were not sure where it would lead. For some young people the route is a stepping stone up to a higher level education and training but for too many it represents an early and undistinguished exit from the education system. The likely labour market destinations of students on these three different pathways are very different.

Almost all of those taking A levels and many taking general vocational programmes at Level 3 will now go into higher education or some form of tertiary education. For this group the employment prospects are still relatively good, although they may be declining in absolute terms. Tertiary educated adults are not all securing graduate jobs— in fact a recent analysis from the Chartered Institute of Personnel and Development,[43] based on European Social Survey data, suggests that between 2004 and 2010 58.8 percent of UK graduates were not in graduate jobs—the third highest rate after Greece and Estonia for all the countries in the survey. However, graduates still do considerably better on the labour market than those with lower level qualifications. OECD estimates for 2011 show that tertiary educated adults across the OECD countries earn on average 1.5 times as much as those with education only to upper secondary level.[44] This wage premium applies to both tertiary Type A (general) and tertiary Type B (vocationally oriented) graduates. Men in OECD countries with Type B tertiary education earn on average 26 percent more than those with only upper secondary education and women 32 percent more. Tertiary educated adults in the UK had a wage premium at the average for OECD countries. For most OECD countries these wage returns to tertiary graduates held up during the 2000s, but in a few countries, including the UK and New Zealand, there was a slight decline between 2000 and 2011.

Those on the higher vocational pathway will either go into tertiary education or enter the labour market directly and, in either case, are relatively better positioned to acquire good jobs than less qualified people. For those with a vocational Level 3 qualification as their highest qualification the wage returns are positive on average but quite variable depending on the qualification. Using LFS data for 2007, one study estimates that the wage returns to those with NVQ 3s, compared to those with only Level 2 qualifications, is 13 percent for males and 10 percent for females.[45] The returns for City and Guilds Level 3 qualifications are similar. However, some vocational Level 3 qualifications, such as BTEC and ONC/OND, shower higher returns. A later study finds average wage gains for holders of Level 3 vocational qualifications, compared to similar individuals qualified only to Level 2, of 10 percent for an NVQ Level 3, 16 percent for RSA Level 3 and 20 percent for a BTEC Level 3.[46]

Those on the lower status Level 2 route have much poorer job prospects. Level 2 vocational qualifications show much lower wage returns. According to one study, the return for those with NVQ 2 as their highest qualification, compared to those with only Level 1 qualifications, is nil for males and only three percent for women, although BTEC, City and Guilds and RSA Level 2 qualifications show somewhat higher returns. Likewise, another study finds that the wage return for those with Level 2 vocational qualifications, compared to similar individuals with qualifications below Level 2, is one percent for those with NVQ Level 2, 12 percent for those with BTEC Level 2, and 16 percent for those with RSA Level 2.[47]

EDUCATION AND JOBS: THE DECLINING VALUE OF QUALIFICATIONS ON THE LABOUR MARKET

Like their parents' generation, young people today are a far from homogenous group. Their lives are shaped by the different barriers and opportunities which they face according to their gender and ethnicity and social class background. This is reflected in the very different routes they take though an upper secondary education system in England which is exceptionally segmented.[48] Compared to their parents' generation, all groups have, on average, received more years of schooling and gained higher level qualifications but this does not necessarily translate in better job prospects.

Our own research comparing occupational destinations of people qualified to different levels in the mid 1980s and in the late 2000s, suggests

Table 2.1 Occupational destinations by level of qualifications: 28–32 years, 1992

	Professional and managerial (%)	Associate professional and technical (%)	Clerical and craft (%)	Semi and unskilled and other (%)	Unemployed (%)	Inactive (%)	Missing (%)	Total % in each qualification level (%)
Tertiary	42.7	26.1	9.2	8.5	3.3	8.9	1.2	20.5
Upper secondary	16.4	8.1	33.4	21.9	7.7	11.1	1.4	21.2
Apprenticeship	8.5	5.0	35.2	28.0	10.8	11.3	1.3	5.3
Lower secondary	13.1	4.3	28.4	26.6	6.0	20.4	1.1	21.7
Below Level 2	4.4	1.0	15.8	31.7	13.1	32.6	1.4	28.1
Other qualifications	9.8	4.6	14.8	37.4	10.7	21.9	0.8	3.0
Missing	0.0	5.3	21.1	31.6	10.5	15.8	15.8	0.2
Total % in each occupational category	17.1	8.7	21.9	23.7	8.2	19.1	1.3	12.17

that there has been a decline in the occupational status on average for people qualified at each level. Using data from the Labour Force Surveys, we looked at occupational destinations at 28–32 years of age by qualification level, in 1992 and 2015. We took 28–32 year olds since this is an age when most are likely to have reached a relatively stable career path, if they are going to at all. The 28–32 samples were divided into those with qualifications at five different levels: tertiary, upper secondary (NQF Level 3), apprenticeship, lower secondary (NQF Level 2) and below Level 2. Apprenticeship is taken as a separate category because of the discontinuities in what constitutes a completed apprenticeship between the 1980s, when most apprenticeships led to a qualification equivalent to what today would be classified as Level 3, and the 2000s when some 70 percent of apprentices only qualify at Level 2. We use a simple classification of occupational destinations into: (1) Professional and Managerial; (2) Associate Professional and Technical, (3) Clerical and Craft, and (4) Semi- and Unskilled. For reporting purposes here we combine (1) and (2) into a single category of 'graduate jobs'. The full data are shown in Tables 2.1 and 2.2 below.

Our analysis shows that amongst 28–32 year olds at each level of qualification occupational status declined overall between 1992 and 2015. This is most evident in the proportion of those qualified to each level who find themselves in semi- and unskilled jobs at age 28–32. The proportion rose between 1992 and 2015 from 8.5 to 14.7 percent for graduates; from 21.9 to 32.9 percent for those qualified to upper secondary level; and from

Table 2.2 Occupational destinations by level of qualifications: 28–32 years, 2015

	Professional and managerial (%)	Associate professional and technical (%)	Clerical and craft (%)	Semi and unskilled and other (%)	Unemployed (%)	Inactive (%)	Missing (%)	Total % in each qualification level (%)
Tertiary	44.5	18.2	12.1	14.7	1.8	8.6	0.1	44.7
Upper secondary	11.7	15.1	25.3	32.9	3.1	11.6	0.3	16.3
Apprenticeship	5.7	2.9	45.0	34.3	4.3	7.9	0.0	2.3
Lower secondary	8.2	11.4	21.1	33.8	5.7	19.4	0.5	14.6
Below Level 2	4.5	4.8	13.2	38.2	7.9	30.8	0.6	14.5
Other qualifications	5.3	2.8	21.7	45.0	4.2	20.1	0.9	7.2
Missing	9.1	13.6	13.6	9.1	4.5	36.4	13.6	0.4
Total % in each occupational category	24.2	13.3	17.2	26.5	3.7	14.8	0.4	59.8

28 to 34.3 percent for those with completed apprenticeships. Across these groups, an increasing proportion found themselves employed below their level of qualification and skill during this period. For those qualified at the lowest level, the proportion in low skilled jobs at 28–32 years also rose, from 26.6 to 33.8 percent, suggesting that over time fewer of these had been able to progress to jobs beyond their initial qualification levels.

Growing rates of over-qualification and under-employment are most evident amongst graduates. Whereas 68.8 percent of graduates in 1992 progressed into 'graduate jobs' by age 28–32, only 62.7 percent did so in 2015. Of those who did not, a larger proportion now found themselves in craft and clerical jobs (12.1 compared to 9.2 percent), and a much larger proportion than before were in semi- and unskilled jobs (14.7 compared to 8.5 percent). The trend amongst those with highest qualification at upper secondary level is slightly more complex. A slightly larger proportion in 2015 (26.8 percent) than in 1992 (24.5 percent) had progressed to graduate jobs, perhaps because of the rapid expansion of jobs classified as associate professional, and fewer were in craft and clerical jobs (25.3 compared to 33.4 percent), but the major shift was in the substantial rise in the proportion finding themselves in low skilled jobs (from 21.9 percent in 1992 to 32.9 percent in 2015).

The average occupational status of apprentices has also declined overall during the period. Considerably fewer apprentices are now progressing beyond their qualification level (from 13.5 to 8.6 percent) and more end up in semi- and unskilled jobs (from 28 to 34.3 percent). But this does not necessarily represent an increase in 'under-employment' since fewer of the recent apprentices will have reached a Level 3 qualification level than in the 1990s. Also fewer of the former apprentices were now unemployed or inactive (from 22.1 to 12.2 percent). Amongst the least qualified (those with below Level 2) slightly more found their way into graduate jobs than before (19.6 from 17.4 percent) and fewer were unemployed or inactive (from 45.7 to 25.1 percent), the latter trend probably reflecting the increasing proportion of lower qualified women now working, albeit that many of these would be in part-time jobs. But more than before were now in semi- and unskilled jobs (from 26.6 to 33.8 percent).

These inter-generational changes in labour market outcomes for people qualified at different levels are quite substantial but they probably underestimate the real decline in labour market opportunities for young people today for two reasons. Firstly, the sample aged 28–32 mostly entered the labour market before the financial crash of 2008, when conditions were better than for young people entering the labour market after the crash. Secondly, since the LFS records all those working at least one hour per week as employed, the employment figures mask the increasing incidence of part-time working amongst young people, many of whom would wish to be full time jobs. We discuss this in the next chapter.

THE EDUCATION OPPORTUNITY BALANCE SHEET

How can we summarise the intergenerational balance sheet on opportunities for young people in and through education? Opportunities to study for young people today are certainly much better than they were for their parents' generation. There is a greater range of provision and more support from governments for young people to take up these opportunities. Consequently young people have better qualifications than their parents had and inequality of opportunities and outcomes for qualifications appear to have reduced, at least at the upper secondary level. Many young people—and particularly young women and those from immigrant families whose parents had very few educational opportunities in their countries of birth—perceive this as a genuine improvement in opportunities over the generations.

However, in terms of future life chances this is something of a mirage. In the first place, while young people are better qualified and have a broader education than their parents had in many respects, in terms of competences in basic skills they fare no better than their parents and inequalities of opportunities for these skills are now much higher than they were. Education is, of course, not only about developing literacy and numeracy, but these skills do matter, and increasingly so in our digital age. Skills in numeracy are still one of the best predictors of future earnings. In the second place, it is clear that better qualifications amongst today's generation of youth are not necessarily translating into better job prospects. This probably has more to do with changes in the labour market than with the skills of young people themselves, even though the latter, in terms of literacy and numeracy at least, may have improved less than one would have wished.

Over the life course of today's youth, it is likely that those who are best qualified will attain occupational positions and earnings comparable to similarly qualified people in their parents' generation. However, the least qualified and most vulnerable on the labour market, and particularly those without a Level 3 qualifications, will almost certainly fair worse than their equivalents in the parental generation. So in life course terms it is likely that there will have been an overall increase in inequalities in socio-economic opportunities by educational levels amongst this generation compared with their parents' generation. Will this amount to an overall decline between generations in life course returns to education? The predictions of Brown and his co-authors with regards to returns from degrees suggest that this might be the case, but we cannot yet know for sure. The next chapter discusses what the existing data tell us about intergenerational trends in employment for young people.

CHAPTER 3

Young People and Employment: The Age of Uncertainty

There has been a crisis for youth building in many European countries two for decades because of persistently high rates of youth unemployment, particularly in France and many southern European countries. But the recent surge in public concern over the situation for young people in the UK came with the 2007 financial crisis and ensuing recession and austerity. It is widely agreed that young people have been harder hit by the recession than other age groups, with unemployment rising further and pay declining more amongst this age group than any other.[1]

OECD data show unemployment rates of British 16–24 year olds rising from an average of 13.5 percent in 2005–2007 to 18.9 percent in 2009. The ratio of unemployment rates of 16–24 year olds and 25–64 year olds increased from 3.8:1 in 2005–2007 to 3.9:1 in 2009.[2] Unemployment amongst young people continued to rise after 2010, and diverged further from the rates for adults as a whole. A similar pattern of post-2007 divergence between the young and older groups is apparent in wage levels. As Paul Gregg and his co-authors have shown, real wages in the UK for those between 16 and 34 fell between 2008 and 2014 by 12–15 percent.[3] For those aged over 35 wages declined by only five to six percent.

Are these long-term structural changes or cyclical changes in the age-related gaps in unemployment and pay?

The trends in youth unemployment over the medium term—from the early 1980s—suggests a cyclical pattern, with unemployment rates for young people being more sensitive to the ups and down of the economic cycle than those for other age groups.[4] Youth unemployment for those

© The Author(s) 2017
A. Green, *The Crisis for Young People*,
DOI 10.1007/978-3-319-58547-5_3

aged 16–24 rose to a high point during the austerity years of the early 1980s (19.7 percent on average between 1980 and 1984), then dropped down to 14.9 percent during the recovery of the last half of that decade, remaining at between 13.6 and 14.5 percent during the 1990s despite the dot.com bubble burst at the end of that period. Youth unemployment dropped further during the expansionary early years of the 2000s (to 11.1 percent between 2000 and 2004), before rising steadily after 2005 (to 14.1 percent in 2008 and to 18.9 percent in 2009 after the effects of the 2007/2008 crisis had taken hold).

The gap between unemployment rates of young people aged 16–24s and those aged 25 and over tends to be higher when overall unemployment is very high, as during the early 1980s and after 2007. However, another trend seems to have emerged since around 1990. The age gaps in unemployment rates seem to rise even during periods when youth unemployment is declining and overall unemployment is lower (at around 5 percent between 2000 and 2007). Youth unemployment rates declined on average during each of the five year periods from 1990 to 2005, yet the ratio of 15–24 youth unemployment to overall adult unemployment rose throughout, from 1.87:1 in 1990–1994 to 3.95:1 in 2009.[5]

There is also some evidence of a divergence in the pay of younger and older workers that goes back well before the 2007 financial crisis. According to the analysis of data from the Annual Survey of Hours and Earnings by the Intergenerational Foundation, between 1997 and 2013 median gross weekly earnings decreased by 19 percent in real terms for 18–21s and increased by only 2.1 percent for 22–29s. On the other hand, there were increases of 11 percent for 30–39s, 9.9 percent for 40–49s and 24.5 percent for those over 50. In 1997 workers over 50 earned 1.7 times as much as workers aged 18–21 and 1.1 times as much as workers aged 22–29. By 2013 the ratios had risen to 2.6 to one and 1.4 to one.[6] Studies by both Howker and Malik and Willetts also find a growing pay gap between young workers and older workers going back to the 1970s. In 1974 50–59s earned four percent more than 25–29s. By 2008 they earned 35 percent more.[7]

Our own analysis using Labour Force Survey (LFS) data from 1984 to 2014 also shows youth unemployment following a cyclical pattern, with declines for both males and females aged 20–29 from the high point in 1984 until 2004, followed by a new spike after the recession and then a decline towards pre-recession levels. By 2014, unemployment rates for male 20–29 year-olds who had left full-time education had almost fallen back to their 2004 level (8.4 compared with 7.7 percent) but remained high for females (9.9 compared with 6.3 percent)

Table 3.1 Youth labour market outcomes for the adult population after graduating from full-time education, by sex (in %)

	1984		1994		2004		2010		2014	
	M	F	M	F	M	F	M	F	M	F
Labour market status										
Employed	80.7	58.7	79.2	65.1	84.1	70.3	82.5	67.4	84.8	67.1
Unemployed	15.4	9.7	14.6	7.3	7.0	4.7	10.0	7.5	7.8	7.3
Inactive	3.8	31.5	6.2	27.6	8.9	25.0	7.5	25.1	7.4	25.5
Current employment										
Working hours										
Full-time (>30 hr)	97.7	79.7	95.9	74.6	93.6	73.7	90.3	69.9	87.8	67.5
Part-time (20–30 hr)	1.5	8.1	2.0	9.7	3.4	12.6	5.0	13.2	7.0	15.5
Part-time (<20 hr)	0.1	12.2	2.1	15.8	2.9	13.7	4.7	17.0	5.2	17.0
Underemployment	1.2	3.7	2.2	5.4	2.1	3.1	4.2	6.0	7.0	8.2
Job type										
Temporary	5.5	7.1	6.2	8.0	5.8	7.7	8.2	7.5	6.5	7.2
Zero hour contract					0.1	0.1	0.7	0.6	2.2	4.2
Precarious					7.7	10.3	11.6	12.9	13.6	17.0
Unemployment										
Unemployment rate	16.0	14.2	15.6	10.1	7.7	6.3	10.8	10.1	8.4	9.9
Long-term unemployment rate	13.2	10.3	10.0	5.0	2.7	1.6	5.5	3.9	4.3	3.7

Base: ages 20–29. Current employment figures refer to the employed subsample. Unemployment figures refer to the labour force. Data from 2nd quarter for 1994, 2004 and 2014. Data from direct respondents only. Weighted averages
Labour Market Status: Break between 1984 and 1994. ILO definitions from 1994 onward
Working hours based on usual working hours
Underemployment: working less than 30 h AND (no ft job available OR looking for an additional job OR looking to replace current job with ft job)
Precarious: Indicator if individual is underemployed, on a temporary contract OR on a zero hours contract
Long-term unemployment rate: % of people who have been unemployed for more than 6 months

(See Table 3.1). 20-25 year olds had higher rates of unemployment than 25–29 year olds throughout the time period. At the peak in 1984 the unemployment rate was at 17.2 percent for those aged 20–25 (13.1 for 25–29s), before declining to 9.7 percent in 2004 (5.2 for 25–29s). The rate for 20–25s soared to 14.5 two years after the start of the last recession (8.2 percent for 25–29s) then dropped back to 11.6 percent by 2014 (7.8 percent for 25–29s) (See Table 3.3).

However, for some measures of precarious working we find evidence of longer term structural change, particularly among the 20–25 age group.

Part-time working has increased significantly amongst young employees since 1984, even if we remove students from the sample (See Table 3.1).

Table 3.2 Youth labour market outcomes by age including students (in %)

	1984		1994		2004		2010		2014	
	<25	≥25	<25	<25	<25	≥25	<25	≥25	<25	≥25
Labour market status										
Employed	67.1	68.3	62.1	72.8	65.3	78.4	60.9	76.1	61.9	76.8
Unemployed	14.2	10.3	12.3	8.6	7.2	4.3	11.0	6.9	9.1	6.5
Inactive	18.7	21.3	25.5	18.6	27.5	17.3	28.1	17.1	29.0	16.7
Current employment										
Working hours										
Full-time (>30 hr)	93.0	86.6	83.5	83.3	74.9	83.0	69.7	79.9	65.2	79.0
Part-time (20–30 hr)	3.3	5.4	5.7	6.4	9.0	8.6	10.2	9.1	13.8	10.6
Part-time (<20 hr)	3.7	8.0	10.8	10.4	16.1	8.3	20.1	11.	20.9	10.5
Underemployment	2.6	1.9	5.5	3.2	3.8	2.2	7.9	3.9	12.5	5.5
Job type										
Temporary	7.1	5.9	10.7	5.9	10.5	5.7	13.8	6.1	11.2	6.4
Zero hour contract					0.2	0.1	1.2	0.5	7.3	2.0
Precarious					13.7	7.5	20.8	9.6	25.9	12.2
Unemployment										
Unemployment rate	17.5	13.1	16.6	10.6	9.9	5.2	15.2	8.3	12.8	7.8
Long-term unemployment rate	13.6	10.1	9.3	5.9	2.4	1.7	5.7	4.0	4.8	3.4
In FT education										
% in education	7.3	1.9	17.8	3.4	24.0	5.0	29.0	7.5	27.3	5.9
% of students in employment	20.6	29.0	28.0	42.0	38.6	37.4	37.7	47.5	35.2	43.4

The proportion of employed 20–29 year old men (who had left full-time education) who were working less than 30 hours per week increased by 10.6 percentage points, from only 1.6 percent in 1984 to 12.2 percent in 2014. For young women the proportion increased by 12.2 percentage points, from 20.3 to 32.5 percent. The largest increases for both groups were in the last decade. In most of the years young men were more likely to work 20–29 hours per week than less than 20 hours per week, but for young women it was the other way round. Breaking it down to those aged 20–24 and those aged 25–29, it is clear that rises in part-time working overall have been considerably greater in the younger age group (See Table 3.3). Between 1984 and 2014, the proportion of employees working part-time rose from 6.7 to 27.3 percent amongst the younger age group (or, as shown in Table 3.2, to 34.7 percent per cent if we include

Table 3.3   Youth labour market outcomes for the adult population after graduating from full-time education, broken down by age (in %)

	1984		1994		2004		2010		2014	
	<25	*≥25*	*<25*	*<25*	*<25*	*≥25*	*<25*	*≥25*	*<25*	*≥25*
Labour market status										
Employed	70.6	68.8	68.2	73.0	71.8	79.2	68.7	76.9	70.2	77.5
Unemployed	14.6	10.3	13.3	8.6	7.7	4.3	11.6	6.9	9.2	6.6
Inactive	14.8	20.8	18.5	18.3	20.5	16.4	19.7	16.2	20.6	15.9
Current employment										
Working hours										
Full-time (>30 hr)	93.3	86.6	86.7	83.4	82.3	83.5	77.4	80.8	72.8	79.7
Part-time (20–30 hr)	3.3	5.4	5.5	6.4	8.1	8.4	9.7	9.0	13.2	10.4
Part-time (<20 hr)	3.4	8.0	7.9	10.3	9.5	8.1	12.9	10.2	14.1	9.9
Underemployment	2.5	1.9	5.3	3.2	3.5	2.1	7.9	3.8	12.3	5.4
Job type										
Temporary	6.5	5.8	9.2	5.8	8.8	5.6	11.9	5.7	9.0	5.8
Zero hour contract					0.1	0.1	1.0	0.5	5.7	2.0
Precarious					11.8	7.3	18.8	9.0	22.7	11.7
Unemployment										
Unemployment rate	17.2	13.1	16.3	10.6	9.7	5.2	14.5	8.2	11.6	7.8
Long-term unemployment rate	13.6	10.1	9.8	6.0	2.6	1.8	6.0	3.9	4.9	3.4

students) and from 13.4 to 20.3 percent amongst the older group. The largest increases for both groups occurred between 2004 and 2014.

The proportion of young people in what might be considered as 'precarious work' more generally has also increased since 2004 (See Table 3.1). Using an indicator that combines non-student employees who are under-employed (working less than 30 hours per week involuntarily) and/or on temporary contracts, and/or on zero hours contracts, we can see that between 2004 and 2014 precarious working rose from 7.7 to 13.6 percent amongst 20–29 year old male employees and from 10.3 to 17 percent amongst female employees of the same age. The rates are higher again for the younger age group. Precarious working rose between 2004 and 2014 from 11.8 to 22.7 percent for employees between 20 and 24 and from 7.3 to 11.7 percent for employees of 25 and above (See Table 3.3).

Table 3.4 Prevalence of precarious working by level of education

Highest level of education	2004	2010	2014
NQF level 4 and above	10.4	13.9	13.9
NQF level 3	6.4	9.0	12.4
Trade Apprenticeships	5.9	9.9	6.0
NQF level 2	7.1	10.4	21.5
Below NQF level 2	7.5	13.6	21.0
Other qualifications	18.2	19.1	15.2
No qualifications	12.4	9.7	28.0

If we include those working in short-term self-employed jobs, the proportion of young people in precarious work may be even higher. Using a slightly wider age base, including 18–29 year olds, Will Hutton estimates that 40 percent were working in part-time, temporary or short-term self-employed jobs in 2014, three quarters of a million more than were in the same position 20 years ago.[8] The recent rises in precarious working are thus very substantial, although they have not perhaps reached the levels suggested by theorists of the rising 'precariat'.[9] Young people with no more than Level 2 qualifications are particularly likely to be in precarious jobs (See Table 3.4) at 42.5 percent in 2014.

A slight upward trend in precarious working applies across the adult population,[10] but there is a more pronounced trend amongst young people, and particularly amongst young women and the less qualified. We found that the proportion of employees aged 20–29 (who had left full-time education) in part-time work increased between 1984 and 2014 by 10.6 percentage points for males, from 1.6 to 12.2 percent, and by 12.2 percentage points for females, from 20.3 to 32.5 percent. Using data from Skills and Employment Survey, also for those working under 30 hours per week, Warren and Lyonette found that between 1986 and 2012, the proportion of all adult employees working part time increased by seven percentage points for males, from two to nine percent, and by only two percentage points for females, from 40 to 42 percent.[11] The shorter time period observed by Warren and Lyonette (26 compared with 30 years) may explain some of the difference in their results for all employees and ours for young employees. Nevertheless, there does appear to be a growing gap for men between young employees aged 20–29 and older employees in rates of part-time working. Older women are still more likely than younger women to be working part-time, because more will be looking after young children, but the difference is reducing.

The overall gap is most pronounced for the youngest employees aged 20–24. Taking young men and women together, the proportion of employees of this age (excluding students) working part-time rose 20.7 percentage points, from 6.7 percent in 1984 to 27.4 percent in 2014. This compares with a rise of around eight percentage points for men and women of all ages between 1986 and 2012 in the Warren and Lyonette analysis.

The proportion on temporary contracts has gone up slightly for both adult employees as a whole and for younger employees. But it probably doesn't make sense to compare the rates for younger and older employees, since for the latter this includes a considerable number of highly paid executives and consultants who are likely to be on fixed term contracts, whereas in the case of younger employees temporary contractual status is unlikely to be compensated for by high remuneration. It should be noted that most of the growing number of agency workers are young. 65 percent of agency workers are under 35.[12]

The evidence on employment status and pay trends since the 1980s does seem to point towards a medium-term decline in employment opportunities for young people. For much of this period, at least from 1984 to 2004, unemployment rates for young people were declining from their previous peak in the early 1980s, and the lower levels reached by early 2000s may be again resumed after the large hike after 2007. However, the middle-term trend towards lower unemployment may have been replaced by a new trend towards greater under-employment, as Wolfgang Streeck has argued to be the case across OECD countries, with a continuous shift towards higher rates of involuntary part-time working.[13] In 2014, amongst employees in their 20s who had graduated from full-time education, seven percent of males reported being under-employed, compared with only 1.2 percent in 1984, and 8.2 percent of females against 3.7 percent in 1984. Since at least 1997, pay for 18–21 years olds has been declining in real terms, while it has been stagnating for those between 22 and 29.

There is also evidence of a divergence in young and older worker pay and working conditions, going back to the 1970s in the case of pay, and to the 1980s in terms of under-employment. The recession from 2008 exacerbated both, but the origins of the divergence seem to go much further back. The baby boomer generation mostly entered the labour market before this divergence took off in the late 1970s, but the cohorts born after them seem to have faced an increasing disadvantage when they entered the labour market compared with older people then and their own age group 30 years before.

These generational differences in working conditions also apply even before young people start earning. The process of finding a suitable job is much more demanding for young people today than it was in the 1960s or even in the 1970s and 1980s. It is not just that young people have to do more to present themselves as 'competitive' in applications and interviews, with ever more time spent honing and circulating impressive CVs which demonstrate distinctive achievements in both academic and extra-curricula areas. It is also because for entry to many jobs now—and particularly for professional jobs—it is necessary to show substantial relevant employment experience prior to applying for a paid job. In a 2013 survey 48 percent of employers said that relevant work experience was the most important factor when selecting graduate recruits.[14] One of the easiest ways for employers to ascertain this is to recruit from amongst those who have already worked for the firm as an intern. The 'Fair Access to Professional Careers' report in 2012[15] estimated that over a third of graduate vacancies will soon be filled by applicants who have already worked for the employer as an undergraduate, many unpaid. The result is that more and more young people find it necessary to take undertake internships, often unpaid, and sometimes serially, in order to break into professional jobs. Research from the Sutton Trust shows that 31 percent of graduates report having worked in such apprenticeships without pay.[16]

Undertaking short periods of work experience during study is not an entirely new phenomenon. Some undergraduates with connections and access to interesting opportunities have traditionally spent a vacation or two gaining such experience. The difference now is that the practice has become virtually mandatory for breaking into some of the professions and is more frequently quite extended and unpaid. Whereas work experience used to be just a few weeks to get a feel of working in a particular work environment, thus helping career decisions, the modern internship often lasts more than six months and can be quite intensive.

This is creating an increasing barrier to social mobility for young people who do not have parents supporting them and who cannot afford to work unpaid for long periods of time. The barriers are particularly high for those wishing to enter the creative and other professions based primarily in London where rents and living costs are so high. If your

parents have a house with a spare room in London and will provide for your keep, working as an unpaid intern for six months or even a year may not pose such a problem. But to others who have to pay their own way it can present formidable barriers, particularly when it turns out that a single internship is not enough and you need to take serial unpaid jobs before you finally land a paid job in your chosen profession. A recent YouGov poll, commissioned by the National Union of Students, found that some 100,000 young people were currently doing unpaid internships. Not surprisingly, some 43 percent of those polled reported that the normalisation of this practice represented a major barrier to finding employment.[17]

Young People's Perceptions of Their Employment Opportunities and How They Compare with Those of Their Parents

For the current generation of school leavers a paradoxical situation arises where opportunities in education seem better than for older generations whereas opportunities for adult careers and lifestyles appear more limited.[18] This is quite consistently reflected in the stories told by our interviewees.

Most young people perceive there to be more educational opportunities for them than their parents, although their views are sometimes qualified and ambiguous. Young people we spoke to typically believed that they benefitted from a wider range of study options than their parents and received more encouragement to continue in study after lower secondary school. Many felt that they were less subject than their parents to limiting normative expectations based on gender and social class. Most likely to see their opportunities as better than their parents were young women and young people whose parents emigrated from developing countries where educational opportunities were more limited. But the perception was widely held by other groups too.

Jessica, a white British nursing graduate, did a Child Care diploma in college and then took various agency jobs before following the academic route. Her parents had experienced careers in journalism and the police force but had left school after O levels. She felt that there were more educational opportunities and information available to her than to her parents and that her generation received more encouragement to pursue education after 16:

> I just think it's more publicised so people know more about it. Whereas I think when my mum and dad were younger it was more like you had to be super brainy and only the rich kids went. ... Whereas now I think it's really encouraged like all the way through school and college, I think it's well promoted, especially on the TV and media now there's adverts for universities all the time, especially around this time.

Like many of our sample, Alison, a white British undergraduate studying nursing and social work, had taken quite a winding path through further education. She had first studied A levels at college and then switched after one year to a Health and Social Care course which provided her passport to university. She came from a modest background, but nevertheless felt that she had more opportunities to study after school than her mother and had received more encouragement than she had:

> ... she didn't have any opportunities open to her, it was kind of you leave school and unless you had the money to go on to university there wasn't kind of these student finance and loans and things like that, there was limited opportunities. She kind of went into more manual work and hairdressing, that kind of thing, which isn't what she wanted to do. And then ... she started a family and ... she's done the kind of education stuff after we've been born ... I think then you kind of leave school at 16, whereas now you've got college and you've got university and they're encouraging you to stay in longer. I don't think there was anything like that, from my mum's experiences anyway.

Athula, a 21-year-old graduate in Business Management, who had come to England from Sri Lanka aged 10, also saw the upside of her situation by comparison with her parents' generation. She had poor experiences in secondary school but went to a good college where she took A levels and then progressed to university. Athula felt her opportunities had been better than those of her parents because she had not been so constrained by the limited expectations placed on her father, as one of a large and poor family, and on her mother as a girl:

> To be honest they're not really from this place, so back there ... my dad ... just completed the GCSEs and started working because of the family situation.

They were really poor, they had a lot of children and he was one of the eldest. Obviously back home it's the men that work and the ladies sit at home and provide. So he started working at a young age … Yeah, it was totally different. So he worked as a clerical admin or something, and he did move up eventually, but then we came here afterwards because of the war back home. And mum, I think she did her A level and then she stopped because there, after a certain age, women don't go to university. Now this has changed…

For many, though not all, migrants, emigration is all about social mobility. Aamuun, a 19-year-old Somali woman who emigrated to England at 16, was studying a Level 2 course in FE college, supported by an Education Maintenance Allowance. Needing to improve her English after arriving in England inevitably slowed her progress in further education, but Aamuun still believed she had many more opportunities in education than her parents had back in Somalia, where her mother had been constrained by traditional gender expectation and her father by poverty.

… my mum, she got married when she was young. She didn't like me … have options, there's so many options that I don't need to get married even if I choose to. No, continuing my education. … My dad … he wanted to continue his education but he couldn't, he had to help the family.

Polly, a white British woman, had done GCSE re-sits and then A levels in college, also supported by an Education Maintenance Allowance, before doing well in University and gaining a good Chemistry degree. Her parents, on the other hand, had left school early because that is what people in their position were expected to do. Attitudes, she says, were different then.

I know that why my dad just stopped his school is because it was totally expected of him to just go out and get a job and then that was it, like you've got a job and now that's all you're ever going to do. And when my mum was younger as well, she was in care, and she was in like 15 different foster homes by the time she was 18 and stuff and so she had like unsettled education. And I think she left school with like 2 Es, so she didn't have that many opportunities. But she was just fed up with everything then and that's why she went back to university when she was 33 and did her social work degree.

Young women and children of migrants were particularly likely to see intergenerational gains in opportunities, but most young people thought

Interview

the same. However, there were some who also noted where things were tougher for young people today. Many talked about the problems of higher education tuition fees and student debt and also the pressures from having to work at part-time jobs while studying. Their parents' generation had not had to pay fees for full-time higher education, (unless from outside the European Union), and many had received grants to study. But some non-traditional mature students had also worked their way through further and higher education. Rita, a 22-year-old graduate of English Studies, who had taken a traditional Sixth Form College path to university, had parents in both camps and hesitated about whether her generation had it better than her parents:

> ... well I think it was easier because there were no tuition fees or anything, but I think my dad had to like work night shifts and be writing his thesis, and sort of like funding himself through uni. So I think in that sense it was harder. But for my mum, she trained to be a teacher for free I think probably, so it was easier in that sense.

This sense of increasing freedom and choice available in the context of education is also relevant in the context of more generally individualized biographies. However, the interviews highlight another side of this story: whether young people felt that educational opportunities may have increased they viewed their chances in the labour market as more limited.

Perceptions of Job Opportunities

> Back in their day, if you went to university I think it was seen as like a big thing, you know, like you had to be quite smart and everything. But nowadays I think everyone pretty much goes to university, and I think doing your Masters is more like getting a degree back then, if you know what I mean?

Here Jake, one of the young men we spoke to, makes a point about the changing values of education and its decreasing potential for more secure labour market outcomes. Although most of our young people thought they had it better in education than their parents, they were also keenly aware that this might well not lead them to better jobs and lifestyles. Many of the young people we spoke to thought that their job prospects were worse now, that there were fewer jobs available to the unqualified, and that qualifications generally were worth less on the labour market. Whatever their level of education, our young people tended to think that jobs were harder to get now than had been the case their parents.

Many graduates we spoke to compared their prospects negatively with previous generations of graduates. Susan, a white British woman, was completing a masters in international law and contemplating a Ph.D. and academic career, but still considered her prospects worse than when her parents graduated. 'It sounds like a degree was worth a lot more then,' she says, 'like if you finished university then you'd get a graduate job and it wouldn't be a problem. Like my mum said, you know, she was offered various jobs.' Now, Susan says: 'it is very different.' Ross, another white British graduate, with a masters in IT and also with well-educated parents, had a similar perspective:

> Well with education it could have been a little bit harder, but in terms of work I'd say there was more work for them then because the economy was in an up period rather than a down period, as in now. So I would say it's a bit easier in a way for them to find a job that they may have wanted.

Many of our interviews with graduates pointed at the decreasing value of 'the degree' in the current labour market, exemplifying the argument we made before about the inflation of qualifications. Humera, a 21 year old British born Pakistani, had a degree in Psychology but was currently working in a shop. In conversation with her father, a graduate engineer, both had agreed that his opportunities had been better.

> I think as soon as he graduated he actually got married, but the thing is that he got a job in what he studied like literally straightaway. And he said to me himself, he goes "the amount of jobs that were there for graduates ..." it was so many, you know, compared to right now ...

The struggle that graduates have to face in the labour market affected the educational choices of some of our respondents. Tracy, a white British woman, got an HND in Childcare through her apprenticeship in a nursery, but she had decided not to go to university because in her view it was more difficult for graduates now:

> I mean competition is a bit harder because most people are going to university now, and due to the recent economic climate there's not as many

unskilled entry jobs available, so that's sort of why there's a lot of people unemployed.

Non-graduates we spoke to, including those with well regarded vocational qualifications, also tended to think their job prospects worse than for their parents' generation. Stephen, a white British man from a working-class family, had gained a Level 3 City and Guilds qualification in Fabrication Engineering through an apprenticeship with a firm he still worked for. Reflecting on whether he had better opportunities than his father he said:

> No I don't think so, I think you could not do quite so well in school and still manage to come out with a job, whereas I think now it is quite critical because people do want to see your qualifications.

Tom, a white British 22 year old with few qualifications, is currently unemployed. He thinks his life is tougher for him than it was for his father.

> Dad found getting jobs dead easy. He used to work when he was like 12 and stuff ... So yeah, there were less regulations and stuff. Education wise I don't think they had the same opportunities you get these days, but I think it was easier to get into industry back then and stuff like that.

A Temporary Dislocation or a Long-Term Trend?

Despite being better qualified than their parents, young people today in many ways face worse prospects in the labour market than did people of the same age 30 years ago. They are certainly more disadvantaged relative to their older contemporaries than was the case then. So how should we assess this in terms of generational change?

It is possible that this relative disadvantage for those in their 20s now represents merely a delayed transition to stable employment patterns. This cohort of young people may catch up with more normal patterns of career progression in time. If the subsequent cohort follow the same pattern, then age-related inequalities will have risen to a new higher norm, but there would have been no marked generational shifts in lifetime employment opportunities. On the other hand, if those now in their 20s carry their relative disadvantages through into middle age, we are seeing more of a cohort effect, whereby a particular generation, coming of age under difficult economic circumstances, and hobbled with student debt and huge mortgages, suffers a lifetime reduction in employment and lifestyle opportunities compared with the generation which preceded them. Such a perspective is implied in the growing literature on the decline in graduate opportunities, whereby the current generation of graduates is less likely than their parents generation to reap the high rewards of professional employment, partly because the supply of graduate skills begins to outstrip demand, and partly because of the rise of the 'high skills, low pay jobs' caused by increased global competition amongst graduates and what Brown and his co-authors call 'digital Taylorism'.[19]

On this scenario, the Millennial generation would be the first since records began to do worse over its lifetime than previous generations. A recent report by the Resolution Foundation[20] uses data from the UK Annual Survey of Hours and Earnings, adjusted to 2016 prices, to track the median pay of five generations as they moved through their working lives. Each generation fared substantially better than the previous one until the Millennial generation. The so-called 'Greatest Generation', born around the time of WW1 (1911–1925), came of age in the wake of the deep post-war spending cuts in the mid 1920s which were followed by the Great Recession of 1929–1934 when they were entering the labour market. They benefitted from the recovery in the second half of the 1930s but soon after found themselves fighting in WW2. Theirs was hardly a lucky generation, but they would undoubtedly have done better overall than the previous generation for which we don't have earnings data. These were born at the end of the 19th Century, fought in WW1 during their youth and, if they survived the war and subsequent global flu epidemic, lived most of their adult lives during the recessionary inter-war years, only for many to be faced with another world war in their middle years.

The so-called 'Silent Generation,' born 1926–1945, did considerably better than the previous 'Greatest' generation. The early ones grew up during the war years and subsequent austerity but joined the labour force at the beginning of the economic expansion from the late 1940s. Like the later members of their generation, although to a lesser extent, they saw some of the benefits of the post-war expansion that so advantaged the baby boomers. Their real median salaries in their 50s were around 25 percent higher than those for the previous generation. Then came the baby boomers (born 1945–1965), who saw the largest generational increase in earnings which peaked in their late 40s at about 40 percent more than the median earnings for the previous generation at the same age. Generation X (born 1966–1980) in turn earned considerably more than the previous baby boomer generation in their early careers but as they hit the recession saw their advantage over the boomers vanish by age 40. Lastly come the Millennials, for whom we only have earning data until their late 20s. As the Resolution Foundation analysis shows, at no point in their early life cycle do they do better than the preceding Generation X against whom they loose ground as they approach 30 years at the time of the financial crisis. According to the Foundation's analysis the typical Millennial working through their 20s has earned £8000 less than a typical person in generation X.

So far this generation has been the first since the generation born at the end of the 19th century to start their working lives worse off than the previous generation. Whether they will catch up during their life course depends entirely on the economic conditions they face which we cannot predict with any certainty. However, the current trends look ominous. For the foreseeable future most economists predict as the most likely scenario a long period of slow economic growth in the UK. This results from the UK's long-term problem of slow productivity growth, due to the low levels of company and state investment, and now from the uncertain trading conditions post-Brexit. All of this is in the context of a gradual eastward shift in the centre of gravity of the global economy.[21] New technological break-throughs may change this picture in the longer term, but for the Millennials trying to make their way up the earnings ladder after a poor start, the picture looks relatively bleak. At the least it seems possible that in generational terms average Millennial earnings will continue to lag as they move into the early middle age, when catching up may prove very difficult in a likely context of widespread technologically-driven job loss.

An alterative reading would be that what we are seeing is not so much a generalised shift for an entire cohort, but more of a polarisation of opportunities. The most fortunate of this cohort, with high levels of education in the more elite universities and strong parental support, at least maintain, if not improve on, the real income levels that their parents enjoyed over the life course. But those with lower qualifications and less social capital have greatly reduced opportunities, and fare much less well than those with similar skills in the previous generation.

The account is lent support by what we know of the long-term changes in the labour market. In the most developed countries, demand for high-skilled employees is expanding, although not necessarily quite as fast as the supply of graduates. At the top end of the high-skilled job market, remuneration rises continually, and for the best qualified amongst graduates, coming from elite universities and with degrees in the most sort after subjects, opportunities get better. Jobs requiring intermediate skills, particularly production and craft skills in the manufacturing sectors, are declining, thus hollowing out the occupational structure. And many of white collar jobs at intermediate skills levels are now taken by graduates unable to find work in graduate professions. At the low skills end of the labour market jobs are certainly not disappearing—although many of the more routine jobs are being automated—because many low skilled service jobs, like caring jobs, cannot easily be automated. But in the long term low skilled jobs are in relative decline, and job quality is diminishing. Since the remaining low skilled jobs not subject to automation can now be so easily outsourced to countries with cheaper labour costs, and because those that remain suffer declining protection from state regulation and trade unions, wages and conditions in low skilled sectors continue to deteriorate, particularly in countries with so-called flexible labour markets. So the opportunities for the best and least qualified continue to diverge.

This scenario does not necessarily suggest that the current generation as a whole will be worse off than their parents through the life course, although opportunities within and between age groups will have become more unequal. However, even if there is no intergenerational life course decline in average earnings, life styles may still deteriorate intergenerationally because other key costs are rising, not least in housing and welfare provision. In the next chapter we look at the intergenerational aspects of the housing crisis. In later chapters we consider the effects of intergenerational transfers in welfare and private pension costs.

CHAPTER 4

Britain's Housing Disaster and Its Effects on Young People

No issue has come to define the Millennial generation, and their blasted hopes, more than housing. For previous generations, going back until the 1970s when the late baby boomers came of age, housing proved to be a major source of wealth accumulation and 'lifestyle mobility', if not for all, then at least for a majority. If social mobility were measured in intergenerational changes in consumer power, then housing asset accumulation would have been counted a major engine of mobility both for baby boomers, and for the X Generation (born 1965–1979) that followed them. For the Millennial generation, by contrast, the protracted housing crisis has proven to be the major barrier to their life chances, and the main symbol of intergenerational declines in opportunity. Whereas young people in the previous generation had an odds on chance of owning a house by the age of 30,[1] and if not, of renting decent homes at affordable at prices, for today's young people in many parts of the country, the chances of either are becoming increasingly remote.

The underlying causes of the UK's 'housing disaster'[2] are complex and they involve each of the drivers of changing youth opportunities discussed at the outset. Demographics have played their part, since ageing populations increase the demand for housing space, because of the high percentage of older people living alone, many of whom prefer not to downsize their accommodation when one partners dies. Other demographic trends are also contributing to increasing demand. Rising divorce rates and other changes in patterns of family formation and lifestyle choice, have meant than more people live in single-person households

© The Author(s) 2017
A. Green, *The Crisis for Young People*,
DOI 10.1007/978-3-319-58547-5_4

than before (up to 14 percent of the over 16s in 2014).[3] Between 1970 and 2005 the population in Britain increased by eight percent while the number of households increased by 30 percent.[4] Population growth and the declining size of household units increase the demand for homes.

At the same time fewer new houses are being built. Governments and private developers have both been responsible. An average of 308,000 new homes were completed each year between 1951 and 1984, roughly half of them by local councils. At the peak in 1968, 425,000 new homes were completed. But from the early 1980s councils virtually stopped building and private developers failed to fill the gap. Between 1998 and 2009 on average only 191,000 were completed each year.[5] Home building reached a new low in 2012, with less than 100,000 completed, only 31 percent of which for social housing. Local councils built just 2.7 percent of new homes, around 3000, across the UK.[6] Building has recovered has only slightly subsequently, with 139,030 new homes completed in the year to June 2016.[7]

Governments since the 1980s have been increasingly reluctant for the state to be the main supplier of housing and have followed their neoliberal instincts in hoping that the private market would fill the gap. Councils have been obliged to sell existing council homes under Right to Buy and have been prevented from replacing them through caps on their borrowing. After 2007 austerity has made government even more reluctant to finance the building of new homes. On the other hand, developers have often been more interested in building luxury and higher-priced homes than affordable homes that yield a lower profit. What is more, given the historic tendency for the price of land and houses to rise rapidly, developers will often leave their land under-developed, hoping that prices will go higher, thus increasing their profits when they do build. In July 2016 there were 684,000 unfinished building sites with detailed planning permission and building work had not even started on half of them.[8]

However, shortage of supply has not necessarily been the only, or even the main, problem. There is more housing space available now per head of population than at any time in history. In 1931 there were an average of 4.2 people for each dwelling. Now there are 2.3. Research by Rebecca Tunstall shows that the average number of rooms available for each person has increased substantially over the years, from one in 1921, to 1.5 in 1971 and 2.4 in 2011.[9] According to the 2011 census for England and Wales the average household comprised 5.4 rooms and

2.7 bedrooms, with 2.4 rooms per person and 1.2 bedrooms per person. Oxford University social geographer Danny Dorling estimates there were in total 66 million bedrooms in England and Wales for 55 million people, and that given the number of couples sharing a bed, there would have been a 'surplus' of bedrooms of about 22 million.[10] He also calculates that there are currently enough empty properties to house two million people. The Office for National Statistics (ONS) calculated that there were roughly 27.5 million dwellings (excluding long-term vacant houses) and 26.5 million households in 2013.[11]

The problem is not so much that we lack housing stock, but that much of it is in the wrong place and the wrong people are buying it, including foreign investor buyers and buy-to-let landlords. Housing generally has become much more unequally distributed. As the Danny Dorling writes: 'The great housing insecurity of our times has been brought about by a minority becoming hoarders of property, and this hoarding has been encouraged by successive governments.'[12]

Rebecca Tunstall's research shows that housing inequality declined in the middle decades of the 20th century, along with income and wealth inequality generally. In 1921 the richest tenth of households had four times as many rooms per person as poorest tenth, but by 1981 they had three times more.[13] However, the distribution of housing become more unequal again after 1980, along with incomes and wealth. The ratio of rooms per person between the top and bottom deciles increased from 3:1 in 1981 to 3.7:1 in 2001 and to 5:1 in 2011.[14] Growing inequality in access to housing space was not only made possible by increasing income and wealth inequality generally, which allowed richer people to buy very large houses, way in excess of their needs, and for quite a substantial proportion of adults to own second homes (17 percent in the UK at the last count). It was also encouraged by policies amongst successive governments which promoted the idea that housing was a profitable market for speculation, as much as a means to fulfill human needs for shelter, privacy and comfort.

There have been tax privileges for home ownership going back many decades. Until it was cut back in the 1980s and finally abolished in 2000, individual home ownership was strongly encouraged by the provision of tax relief on mortgage interest (MIRAS in its last incarnation). However, what has happened since then is that tax privileges have been directed towards those buying multiple homes to rent for profit. Buy-to-let landlords have received special tax and mortgage terms which have greatly increased the profitability of renting out properties as a business, so that the returns to investing in properties for rent now greatly exceed the normal return on the stock market. A 2014 report by Paragon, one of Britain's leading buy-to-let lenders, found that since 1996 investment in buy-to-let properties had averaged an annual rate of return of 16 percent, far outstripping the return on shares and bonds at 6.8 and 6.5 percent respectively.[15] Even without rents, returns to housing investment have outpaced the average returns to FTSE100 companies over the past 20 years by 7.3 percent compared with 6.3 percent.[16] In fact the increase in the value of property generally has so far exceeded that of the stock market, that Martin Weale estimates that property is now 50 percent over valued compared with stocks.[17]

In addition, housing remains one of the few capital assets that is not subject to capital gains tax (CGT). It is true that second homes are nominally subject to CGT on sale, but the rules are so easily evaded by multiple home owners switching houses temporally—to classify second as first homes before selling—that the provision is more honoured in the breach than the observance. In conjunction with the de-regulation of the private rental market since the 1980s, which makes the exploitation of tenants by landlords much easier, all this has greatly encouraged the notion that investing in residential property is for profit rather than for personal needs. The financialisation of the mortgage lending market since the mid 1980s, with the de-mutualisation of building societies, and the globalisation and de-regulation of banking generally, has also under-written the process of transforming residential property from a matter of home ownership to financial speculation.[18] A new class of landlords has grown on the back of this. According to Savills, landlords with mortgages now have more housing market equity than owner-occupiers with mortgages.[19]

The result of all this has been a seemingly inexorable rise in house prices. Between 1983 and 2007, just before the bubble burst, nominal house prices had risen by a multiple of six, many times faster than wages.[20] For young people buying in the years between 1970 and 1990, first-time buyer home prices had been, on average, at an affordable 2.4 times their average incomes. For those buying between 1997 and 2009 the ratio had risen to a quite unaffordable 3.41 to 1.[21] By 2016 the average home was costing almost eight times average earnings and twice that ratio in London.[22] At their peak in 2007, just before the crash, mortgages for first time buyers were at 3.4 times their average income (suggesting purchasing prices, which generally exceed loans, at almost 4:1).

By 2010 the average deposit was at £56,000, roughly double the average wage.[23] Those who could get mortgages, not surprisingly, tended to borrow at very high loan to value ratios (median advances were at 90 percent LTV), and many had to resort to 'interest-only' deals to make their mortgage payments affordable (24 percent of all loans), thus diminishing their home ownership status to a more secure form of renting.[24]

The effect of all this has been to put home ownership increasingly out of reach for most young people. Not surprisingly, fewer and fewer are buying houses. In 1990, 50 percent of home owners were under 35 year old age. Just 20 years later this fraction had dropped to 29 percent.[25] In 1985, 34 percent of under 25s were already home-owners. This dropped to 19 percent by 2005. Among 25–29 year olds, owner occupation rates were down from 62 percent at their peak in 1985 to 46 percent 20 years later. By 2007 the mean age of first time buyers had risen to 32 and 37 for those without parental assistance.[26] Owner occupation amongst the under 30s was already a minority experience by 2007 but it was likely to become even rarer in the years to come. According to the projections produced by the Joseph Rowntree Foundation, the total number of 18–30 year olds owning their own homes is likely to drop from 2.4 million in 2008 to 1.3 million by 2020. Whereas around 35 percent of 18–30s owned their homes in 1997, only about 25 percent did so in 2008. By 2020 that proportion is predicted to drop to around 12 percent.[27]

If buying has become near impossible for most young people, other alternatives, whether they be social housing or private renting, are equally problematic. Social housing has been declining remorselessly for three decades. In 1980 local councils provided accommodation for 31 percent of the country's households. After the 1980 Housing Act, much of this stock was sold off (at 40–60 percent below market value) under the Right to Buy initiative. With much reduced central government funding for council house building in the ensuing years, councils replaced very few of the 1.85 million council houses sold off,[28] so that by 2008 council tenants made up only 16 percent of households.[29] Housing Association provision failed to take up the slack. The result has been ever lengthening waiting lists for council housing. Young people are least likely to qualify for these occupancies, unless they have dependent children, because they have not had time to advance themselves up the queue, so not many of them get access to this dwindling stock of affordable housing. Whilst 14 percent of 18–30 year olds were in some form of social housing in 1997, only nine percent were so in 2015.[30]

The remaining alternative for young people leaving home has been privately rented accommodation in a sector which had grown rapidly, not least as a result of financial crisis and subsequent restraints on home loans.[31] The proportion of young people renting in the private sector has thus increased substantially, from around 12 percent in 1997, to 28 percent in 2015, and it is projected to rise to 33 percent by 2020.[32] In many countries with better regulated private rental markets this might not be such a bad thing. But the problem for young people forced to rent privately in the UK it that the sector is less regulated than in almost any other country in Europe.[33] Consequently, tenures are insecure, housing quality is often poor, and prices are often excessively high.

According to the National Housing Federation the cost of renting rose a massive 37 percent in the five years to 2012, and it has been going up at a rapid rate since then.[34] In London in 2012 rents rose eight times faster than incomes. By 2012, average monthly rents had reached £744 nationally and £1102 in London. They have continued to rise in London and other cities in southern in England at an astronomical rate. Recent hotspots have been southern university towns like Brighton and Bristol, where rents rose by an average 18 percent in 2015 alone.[35] Many young people are having to spend so much on rent that saving for a deposit an impossibility. Data for 2014/2015 from the English Household Survey show average private tenants paying over half of their household incomes on rent.[36] For young people with lower earnings the proportion would be even higher.

But the high costs of renting are not the only problem. Despite the sky-high rents, the quality of properties is often very poor, with many properties reported as not safe for human habitation. Amongst those interviewed by the British Household Panel Survey in the early 2000s, those in privately rented accommodation were more than twice as likely as owner occupiers to report problems with condensation, lack of adequate heating and damp.[37] Buy-to-let landlords typically have small property portfolios which they maintain alongside other jobs. They are thus part-time and essentially amateurs in the role of renting accommodation, typically knowing less about landlord/tenant law and tenants' rights than traditional landlords.[38] Unfortunately, a proportion of them fail to keep their properties in good repair and at a standard fit for tenants and evidence is emerging that this is increasingly common. The Migrants' Rights Network claims that Ealing may have as many as 60,000 occupants in illegal structures, and Slough, reportedly, has up to 6000 'beds in sheds'. Recently we have seen the rise of 'rent-to-rent' which in some cities is becoming synonymous with multi-occupancy in poor quality dwellings.[39]

According to a recent investigation by Shelter, official complaints against landlords to local authorities rose by 27 percent in the three years to 2012, with a total of 85,000 complaints in the last of those years.[40] Of those complaints, 62 percent were about serious and life-threatening hazards. Tenants most frequently complain of landlords refusing to make necessary repairs. However, when tenants do complain they can find themselves subject to 'revenge evictions' by landlords who presume they can always find another tenant, who will probably pay an even higher rent. The number of evictions by a private landlord has risen by 60 percent over five years from 2010/2011 to 37,000 annually. Over the same period, as the 2016 'Monitoring Poverty and Social Exclusion' report points out, mortgage repossessions have fallen to from 23,000 to 3300.[41]

Not the least amongst the problems faced by renters in the private sector is the extreme level of insecurity they face. Since the de-regulation of the privately rented sector in the 1980s, landlords have been free to evict tenants after a year, in practice for any reason they wish. John Major's 1996 Housing Act introduced the Assured Shorthold Tenancy, allowing tenants and landlord to give notice after just six months. As a result private landlords, spurred on by their agents, have come to believe that they should raise their rents annually and tenants, unable able afford another rent hike, frequently end up moving within the year. The length of tenure amongst those who have the freedom to choose is typically about seven years. The median stay in a dwelling for owner-occupiers is 7.1 years and that for social renters 7.8. In contrast, the median private tenant stays only 1.7 years before moving on.[42] The increasing precariousness of tenures amongst private renters has been associated with higher levels of 'risk' and uncertainty and with associated threats to wellbeing and health.[43] Indeed, the most commonly cited source of the relationship between housing tenure and ill-health in the academic literature is 'ontological insecurity'—the feeling of being unsafe in their world.[44]

For many young people, who still dream of owning their own homes, this is a no-win situation. More and more decide to stay living in the family home, so that they can at least save towards a mortgage deposit. Others, the so-called 'boomerang children,' end up returning to live with their parents after failed attempts at independent living in the private rental jungle. By 2011, 29 percent of males aged 20–34s and 18 percent of women were still living in the parental home.[45] Those who do prolong residence in the family home are more likely to have parents who own houses, and have the space to accommodate them, or alternatively, to have insufficient income to rent privately. Surveys report that they are also more likely to say they are delaying entering long-term relationships and starting families because they can't get their own accommodation.

The current housing crisis, which shows no signs of abating, represents the biggest single barrier to young people getting on with their lives and taking the traditional steps towards adult status. At one level it is a vivid example of the delaying of transitions for young people, and many young people perceive it this way and still hope to be owning homes before too long. A MORI poll in 2016 found that 80 percent of 25–34 year olds would like to be owner occupiers in five years time, if they had the choice, a similar proportion to all adults.[46] However, for many their hopes are unlikely to be fulfilled. Today's young people will carry the burdens of the dysfunctional housing market bequeathed by previous generations with them throughout their lives. The majority may never own their own homes at all, if current trends in declining home ownership continue.

Those that do manage to get on the ladder, will take longer to pay off their mortgages and thus be saddled with higher debts into late middle age, just when they need to be saving for their retirement on meagre pensions. The lucky ones will have inherited from their parents or been gifted funds to buy homes when they were younger. But this is a minority of all young people, with just 27 percent of first-time buyers getting help from family and friends in raising the deposit for a mortgage.[47] Older people are increasingly having to down-size their homes to release equity to pay for health care or to fund their longer retirements. By the end of the 2000s, 30–50,000 properties were being sold each year to pay for care, while 160,000 houses were left in estates annually.[48] Only one in six parents were leaving a house to their children, which suggests that no more than one third of the children's generation were benefiting, and then in most cases not until their middle age. When the current generation of young people reach middle age their parents homes will be even more valuable than they are now, but less of that value will be passed on because more of the parents will have 'spent the inheritance.'[49]

Britain's disastrous housing system is undoubtedly at the heart problem of intergenerational inequalities. The baby boomers and, to a lesser extent, the Xers who followed them, were hugely fortunate as generations. They bought houses when they were relatively cheap, many of them council houses at highly discounted rates; the older ones saw their

mortgage burdens ease rapidly in the inflationary 1970s; and they ending up owning valuable properties which they could use as collateral for
more borrowing and spending in middle age. Many of them could sit
back and watch their property wealth rise inexorably, increasing by more
each year than they were earning from work. Indeed in the South East
of England in 2015 house prices were still rising annually by an average
£29,000—by almost £5000 more than average pay.[50]

The scale of this money making machine was surreal. The value of the
18 million or so homes in the UK rose on average by about £100,000 in
the seven years preceding the financial crisis.[51] If 15 million of their owners were owner-occupiers throughout the decade their collective housing
assets would have grown by about £1.5 trillion. That sum was roughly
equivalent to our annual GDP and considerably more than the UK public
debt. Even netting out for inflation and home improvement costs you can
estimate private gains of over one trillion pounds in that decade alone.[52]
These gains were not going to young people, since in 2008 the under 35s
owned just 3.2 percent of Britain's £2.9 tn of housing stock.[53] These property gains therefore represents a transfer of wealth from the future generation of home-buyers to the existing 35 plus generation of home owners in
the order of magnitude of the 2008 UK GDP in just seven years.

The intergenerational imbalances do not stop there. The inflated rents
paid by young people today are mostly going to older adults. About two
million adults now act as landlords.[53] Many of these are buy-to-let investors, who took 13 percent of all mortgages granted in 2012. Of these
investors, 58 percent were aged 46–65. On the other hand, over half of
all private renters are estimated to be under 35 years.[54] If Britain is fast
returning to an age of rentier capitalism, last seen in the Edwardian era,
as Thomas Piketty maintains, it is the older generations who form the
core of this new class of landlords. And they have been aided and abetted
by governments which under-regulate the private rental market; spend in
excess of £27 bn on housing benefits, much of it going to private landlords, and until 2016, gave special tax privileges to buy-to-let landlords.

With over-heated housing markets, and returns on investment way
above the stock market average, the incentives for this new breed of
amateur landlords are huge. But unfortunately for younger people they
are hiking house prices further, at the same time as reducing the quality
and security of rented accommodation, since it is the amateur landlords
who are least likely to maintain properties. They are also more likely to
want to give notice to tenants because when you own just a couple of

properties you are more likely to want to take back your small rented property at short notice, either because a member of your family suddenly needs housing, or for your own use, because finances have got a bit tight, or to perform the temporary address switch that people with second homes regularly make to avoid paying capital gains tax on the sale of a second home.

INTERGENERATIONAL DECLINE MEETS SOCIAL CLASS POLARISATION

Of all the domains in which young people see their opportunities restricted, housing represents the most serious, and the one which most clearly represents a growing gap between generations in life time opportunities. As they grow older most young people may well catch up with their parents' generation in terms of jobs and earnings. Yet in housing, we are witnessing a genuine divergence in intergenerational fortunes, which will almost certainly affect the majority of the young generation throughout their lifetimes. However, at the same time this generational decline is cross-cut by growing class divisions amongst young people. Housing opportunities are becoming increasingly polarised by social class and social background. In England, where homeownership has been a major vehicle for social mobility for two post-war generations, class polarisation in housing opportunities now works to reduce it.

Analysis of the trends in housing tenure during the medium term show quite clearly that we are experiencing both a substantial social class polarisation in access to the most desirable forms of housing, as well as an overall intergenerational decline. Our own analysis of the trends between 1991 and 2013, using the data from the British Household Panel Survey and its successor Understanding Society, shows not only how far the patterns of tenure amongst young people have changed in recent decades, but also how this has affected young people in all occupational groups. It also shows a stark polarisation in tenure patterns by social group and social background.

Between 1991 and 2013 the proportion of young people aged 18–34 in England owning their own homes almost halved, declining from 46 to 25 percent (See Fig. 4.1). The proportion who were social renters also declined, from 15 to 12 percent. At the same time the proportion living with parent(s) rose from 29 to 42 percent, and proportion renting privately increased from ten to 21 percent. Most of the decline in home ownership

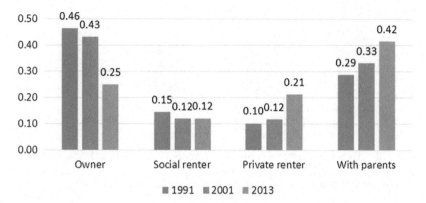

Fig. 4.1 Trends in proportion of 18–34 year olds in England in different tenures, 1991, 2001, 2013. *Source* Calculations from British Household Panel Survey/UK Household Longitudinal Study data: Weighted estimates

happened after 2001, with those who would formerly have bought homes now staying in the parental home or renting privately.

The decline in home ownership amongst young people affected all socio-economic groups. Taking 18 to 34s—reflecting the fact that the most now cannot buy home until their 30s—Fig. 4.2 shows that all groups have experienced declines between 1991 and 2013, mostly occurring in the 2000s. The proportion of young people in professional and associate professional jobs who owned their home dropped by 26 percentage points over this 22 year period, with only half being owners by the end. For those employed in non-graduate jobs the declines were even greater: around 38 percentage points for those employed in skilled (manual or non manual) jobs and 39 percentage points for those in semi- and unskilled jobs. Less than a quarter in the latter category owned their own homes by 2013. The declines in home ownership for those in skilled and semi- and unskilled jobs appear to have started earlier than for those in professional jobs, being apparent already by 2001 when professional home ownership still maintained its 1991 level. However, the decline in home ownership for young professionals was particularly sharp during the house price boom years after 2001 and by 2013 all groups of young people had substantially less chance of owning a home than 22 years previously.

However, whilst this is a generational issue, with all social groups amongst todays' young people less likely to be owners than the earlier

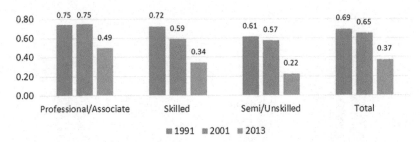

Fig. 4.2 Trends in proportion of home owners by occupational class for 25–34 year olds, 1991, 2001 and 2013. *Source* Calculations from British Household Panel Survey/UK Household Longitudinal Study data: Weighted estimates

generation at the same age, it is also a manifestation of growing inequality. Figure 4.3 shows for different years the odds ratios for owning a house of professionals and associate professionals, and those in skilled jobs, compared with those in semi- and unskilled jobs. In 1991, compared with young people in semi- and unskilled jobs, professionals were 1.85 times as likely to own a home and those in skilled jobs were 1.65 times as likely. By 2013 the odds ratios had increased substantially so that, compared with young people in semi- and unskilled jobs, those in professional jobs were now 3.35 times as likely to own a home and those in skilled jobs 1.78 times as likely. Inequality in home ownership increased across the whole class social spectrum but particularly at the top end.

During the same period, the effect of social background on the chances of young people in England owning a home also increased substantially. Figure 4.4 shows the trends in the odds ratios for owning a home of young people with parents in different occupational groups (when the children were 14 years old). In 1991, compared with young people with parents in semi- and unskilled jobs, those with parents in professional and associate professional jobs were 1.44 times as likely to own a home, and those with parents in skilled jobs were 1.34 times as likely. By 2013, those with parents in skilled jobs were now 1.55 times as likely to own a home as those with parents in semi- and unskilled jobs. The increase over time in the odds ratio was even larger for those from more privileged backgrounds. By 2013, young people whose parents had professional jobs were now 2.39 times as likely to own a home as those whose parents had semi- or unskilled jobs. The estimates for 2001 are not significant, but since the changing patterns of home ownership

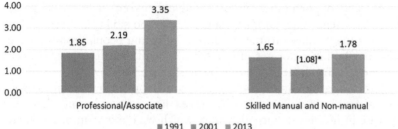

Fig. 4.3   Trends in odds ratios for owning accommodation amongst 25–34s by occupational class. *Source* Calculations from British Household Panel Survey/ UK Household Longitudinal Study data: Weighted estimates. The odds ratios are computed cross-sectionally on the three waves of BHPS-UKHLS : 1991, 2001 and 2013. *Note* *Means that the estimated odds ratio is not significant at the 95 percent confidence level

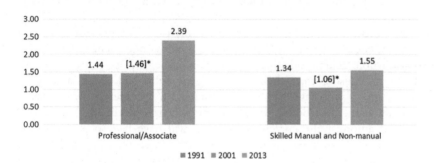

Fig. 4.4   Trends in odds ratios for owning a home amongst 24–34s in England by parental occupational class. *Source* Calculations from British Household Panel Survey/UK Household Longitudinal Study data: Weighted estimates. The odds ratios are computed cross-sectionally on three waves of the BHPS-UKHLS survey, for years 1991, 2001 and 2013. *Note* *Means that the estimated odds ratio is not significant at the 95 percent confidence level

occurred mostly in the 2000s we may assume that these changes in home social background effects on home ownership happened mostly in that period as well.

During a two-decade period when the relative benefits of home owning, compared with renting, have never been bigger, both in terms of quality of tenure and wealth accumulation, we have seen inequalities in housing opportunities almost double between children of professional and semi- and unskilled families. The possibility to own a home is increasingly limited to the third or so of young people from better-off families who inherit or get substantial help with their mortgage deposits. For the rest the chances of home ownership are very low.

As housing mobility has declined, so the gaps in ownership between young people in different social classes has increased. And this sharp increase in housing tenure inequality which we observe amongst todays' young people is likely to persist as their cohort grows older. Indeed, it may well increase as those on higher incomes who have not yet been able to buy a home by age 34 finally manage to get on the housing ladder in middle age, some with help from parental gifts or inheritances, while a large proportion of those on lower incomes, often without the benefit of parental gifts or inheritances, remain permanently excluded. So the housing opportunities for a whole generation, through its life course, will have become more unequal than for the preceding generation during its lifetime.

But growing housing inequality remains only one part of the story of intergenerational changes in housing opportunities. The other side is that a whole generation, throughout its lifetime, will have a worse experience of housing than their parents' generation had. Each socio-economic group will have had to wait longer on average to own a home and the chances of doing so at any age will have declined. Those who succeed amongst the current generation will have had to pay more to buy a home than their parents did, and the price they pay will have a been financial bonus to their parents' generation, which they will be unlikely to inherit in full since their parents will often have used this to fund retirement and care in older age. Because the current generation who buy homes are having to pay such high prices, they will also be burdened with higher debts than their parents throughout most of their lifetimes, which will limit consumption capacity and lifestyle options even when they achieve incomes at comparable levels to their parents in time.

CHAPTER 5

Wealth and Welfare: Breaking the Generational Contract

The opportunities open to today's young people through their lifetimes will depend to a large extent on their prospects in employment and housing. They will assess their fortunes as a generation by how much they can earn and consume relative to the parent's generation, and also by the quality of housing they can afford compared with their parents. These two constitute a major part of what we think of when we compare lifestyle opportunities between generations. However, they are by no means the only factors which determine how one generation fares compared with other generations. Equally important are wealth and how the costs and benefits of state welfare are distributed across age groups and generations.

Wealth

Wealth represents the most visible overall measure by which individuals and families compare themselves with each other and by which we compare different groups in society. It gives access to many of those things which people consider as part of a desirable lifestyle. Both in the media and in society more generally, wealth signifies status and well-being, perhaps more so than at any time since the Edwardian era in Britain. No wonder for the popularity of the recent television drama, Downton Abbey, which chronicles the fortunes of the rich (and their servants) from its apogee in the years before the First World War, to the relative declines after World War Two. The story of the dwindling fortunes of

© The Author(s) 2017
A. Green, *The Crisis for Young People*,
DOI 10.1007/978-3-319-58547-5_5

post-war aristocrats, and the parallel rise of the working class, is, in many ways, well captured, but it is no doubt the sheer scale of opulence of the rich in their glory days which most captivates. As Thomas Piketty has shown, the tables have since turned again, with the rich both more wealthy and more differentiated from the rest than at any time since the first decade of the last century.

Wealth in the UK is very unequally distributed—much more so in fact than earnings or household incomes—and the gaps have been growing since the late 1980s or earlier (depending on which definitions and sources you use). Currently, the top ten percent own more than 100 times the wealth of the least affluent ten percent.[1] According to the data from the ONS Wealth and Assets Survey in 2006/2008, the most reliable source we have, the least wealthy half of households had nine percent of total wealth, whereas the wealthiest 20 percent had 62 percent. Financial wealth is the most unequally distributed, with the wealthiest 20 percent owning 84 percent of assets and least wealthy half owned just one percent.[2] But residential property wealth is also very unequally spread around. Because wealth is mostly inherited not earned—almost three quarters of it currently in the UK—and because substantial inheritance benefits relatively few, it is much more unequally distributed than incomes. The usual measure of the inequality in how things are distributed, the Gini coefficient, would be 100 where just one person owned everything and nought where everyone had equal amounts of wealth. The Gini coefficient for total net household wealth, calculated from the 2006–2008 Wealth and Assets Survey, is 61—almost double that for net household income which, taking into account the size of households, currently stands at 36.[3]

We don't know by exactly how much wealth inequality has risen in recent years: the Wealth and Assets Survey does not provide data on trends in wealth distribution. However, we do know that it has been rising. Piketty's broad brush decennial historical estimates show the share of wealth of the top ten percent in Britain declining substantially for most of the 20th century, from 90 percent in 1910 to around 62 percent in 1975, and then rising again to 70 percent in 2010.[4] The more recent data come partly from HMRC figures on the size of probated estates. These tend to under-estimate inequality because they do not include gifts made more than seven years before death which, being exempt from inheritance tax, represent a common way for those with assets to pass them on to their children. Even so, they suggest that wealth has become much more unequally distributed since 1990. Between 1976 and 1990 there was a small and uneven trend towards lower wealth inequality, although with a spike in 1987 (as measured by the Gini coefficient for 'personal marketable wealth' since the source is individual estates on death). However, since 1991 there has been a substantial increase, with the Gini coefficient rising from 63 to 71 percent in 2002 (before dropping back again to 67 percent in the following year).[5] The overall trend towards rising wealth inequality since 1990 is partly due to the increase in inequality in housing wealth.

Also growing are the inequalities in wealth between different age groups. Wealth is typically accumulated throughout the lifecycle, as individuals gain more possessions, accumulate more in housing assets and savings, and grow their pension entitlements. So older age groups are always wealthier than younger ones, at least until people retire. According to the 2010 report of the National Equality Panel, median household wealth for households with reference persons aged 25–34 was £66,000, compared with £416,000 for those with reference persons aged 54–64 and £172,000 for those with reference persons aged 85 plus. There is, of course, also considerable inequality of wealth within each age group. Amongst the 50–64 age group the bottom ten percent have less than £28,000 on average whereas top ten percent have more than £1.3 million. But the age group differences are equally marked and are also growing. According to Bank of England estimates, between 1995 and 2005 the median net household wealth (not including pensions) of those aged 25–34 dropped 69 percent, from £3000 to £950. For those aged 35–44 it increased by 230 percent from £22,788 to £54,475; for 55–64s by 298 percent from £50,000 to £149,500 and for those over 65 by 241 percent from £39,500 to £95,500.[6]

One of the main reason for this growing inequality of wealth between age groups is housing. The age groups with the largest gains in wealth during the period, the 35–44s and the over 65s, are also the age groups with the largest share of gross housing wealth. Of a total of £3.16 trillion worth of gross national housing assets, the under 35s owned 11 percent, the 35–44s 22 percent and the over 65s 26 percent. We can also see the relationship in the differences in the wealth of people with different housing tenures. In 2006/2008 the median total wealth of outright home owners was £410,000, compared with £269,700 for mortgagees, £24,600 for private tenants and £17,500 for social tenants.[7] The gap between housing rich and housing poor is increasing even as more in the middle have become home owners.[8] This also increases the wealth gaps between the young and older people.

Furthermore inheritance does not seem to be compensating for the rising age inequality in wealth due to housing inequality. HMRC data on probated estates shows that the annual number of estates including housing assets declined between 1969/1970 (149,592) and 1992/1993 (142,446). This is partly because the cohort that own more houses are not yet dying. People aged 30 in 1980 were still only 66 in 2016. The major increase in housing wealth in estates is unlikely to come for another ten years. Also, while it is true that many older people with housing assets are passing part of them on as gifts, it is also true that many baby boomers are 'spending the inheritance' before they die, in many cases to pay for their growing health and social care bills. Inheritance does not compensate the young generation as a whole for its diminishing assets and those that it does benefit are a minority.

According to a 2004 Joseph Rowntree Foundation report 54 percent of those surveyed had never inherited, and of those that did only 11 percent received an inheritance which included property. While over half of home owners had received an inheritance at some point in their lives, less than a third of tenants had. Only 28 percent of those in social class E inherited with only 15 percent receiving more than £10,000.[9] A more recent report from the Institute for Fiscal Studies notes that elderly households are becoming more wealthy. Among households where all members are 80 or over, average non-pension wealth in 2012–2013 was £230,000 compared with £160,000 for the same age group in 2002–2003. However this wealth is very unevenly distributed with the top half of households holding 90 percent of this wealth. Hence, only the 'lucky' half of the children's generation will be inheriting most of the wealth from the older generation.[10] As the report comments, these trends mean that inherited wealth is likely to play an increasingly important part in the life chances of the younger generation. At the same time it looks likely to increase inequalities within this generation with serious negative consequences for social mobility.

As the age-related inequalities in home ownership increase in the coming years, so will the age-related gaps in wealth overall. The declining size of private pensions accruing to younger generations will also add to this effect if we include pension wealth as part of overall total. On current trends, with the gradual eclipse of final salary pension schemes and, in fact, the erosion of private pensions per se, the next generation of young people can expect to be poorer relative to older generations even than today's youth. To what extent does this indicate a lifetime intergenerational decline in wealth and is the trend likely to continue for future generations?

If, as Piketty argues, private wealth is still growing in relation to the overall economy, then it seems unlikely, on current trends, that over their lifetimes the Millennials will amass less wealth overall than their parents' generation, unless of, course, GDP declines. It will just become more and more unequally distributed, across and within age groups. On the other hand, if baby boomers spend more of their wealth in old age, and if policy makers were to decide that the public debt was unsustainable and had to be paid off through large increases in taxation on private wealth and incomes, the Millennial generation could find itself less wealthy than the previous generation through their life course. This all depends on public policy and particularly on policies relating to taxation and social transfers.

INTERGENERATIONAL TRANSFERS

David Willetts estimated (for 2009) that governments currently spent around £125 billion pa in welfare on those over 65 (£50 billion in health care and £75 billion in state pensions). By contrast it spent about £80 billion on people under 18 (£50 billion on education an the rest on child benefits and tax credits). The flow goes increasingly towards the old rather than to the young. The over 60s currently get three quarters of all public spending on benefits. The Treasury's long-term spending projections show the proportion of spending on age-related benefits rising from 20.1 percent of GDP in 2007/2008 to 26.6 percent in 2057/2058. As the current 20s age group reaches their 40s, when they pay most tax, their tax burden may have increased very substantially. Those born in the 2017 will enter their 40s in 2057 by which time total age related government spending may have grown as a proportion of GDP by six percentage points. This suggests much higher taxation for the coming generation when they reach their prime earning years.

Welfare states are designed to smooth the risks over the life course, and they generally involve adults of working age being net contributors and the young and the old being net beneficiaries. However, as populations age, the age-related imbalances tend to get larger, with those in their prime working years being obliged to pay more taxes to fund the health care and state pensions of a larger elderly population. Age-related inequalities in net contribution to the welfare system would have increased, but lifetimes costs and benefits for different generations might not have changed. The so-called generational contract over the welfare state would still be in place. However, if the current young generation make larger contributions in taxes to the welfare state than previous generations in their prime years, but fail to get the same benefits when they retire, the intergenerational contract begins to break down, and a gap will have opened up in the lifetime welfare benefits of two generations.

Historical estimates by London School of Economics social policy expert, John Hills, of what past generations have put in and taken out, does suggest that some generations do better than others. Those born between 1901 and 1921, when the welfare state was just getting established, are estimated to have taken out between 115 and 122 percent of what they put in. Then the balance evened out until the baby boomers. The late baby boomers born between 1956 and 1961 are forecast to get out from the welfare state 118 percent of what they put in.[11] As Willetts suggests, the young people today are likely to be generational losers. This will almost certainly be the case in terms of private pensions, since they will be paying higher contributions during their prime years to fund the growing costs of the relatively generous pensions held by many of their parents' generation. But they themselves may only receive a pittance in retirement from their own 'defined contribution' occupational pensions schemes, if indeed they have them, which many will not. The relatively generous 'defined benefit' pensions schemes of the past are fast becoming extinct, dropping from five million in 1995 to only 500,000 now.[12]

A similar generational inequality may apply in relation to state benefits, as Willetts suggests, since it seems highly unlikely that governments will be able to retain current real-terms levels of spending per retiree on state pensions and healthcare when the number of pensioners reaches one third of the population. There is already growing debate about the so-called 'triple lock' on pensions, which ensures that these always rise faster than incomes and prices. Treasury predictions for the next 40 years suggest that with current policies public spending grows by 4.9 percent of GDP, and this is without factoring in population increases. The estimated costs of NHS rise from five percent of GDP in 1990 to ten percent in 2040. Half of the NHS budget is spent on pensioners, so on these predictions, pensioners' healthcare alone could take up five percent of GDP by 2040.

Is the generational inequality in net contributions to the welfare state limited to a once off imbalance between the baby boomer generation and the later Millennial generation? Willetts's focus is certainly here. However, other projections based on so-called 'generational accounting', suggest that the generational inequalities will not stop there. National Institute of Economic and Social Research economists, McCarthy, Sefton and Weale, produced a set of generational accounts in 2011 which calculated 'the net life-time contribution, positive or negative, that people, as a function of their age, are expected to make to the Exchequer.'[13] Receipts include both welfare benefits and public consumption, which they allocate as far as possible by age. Payments are largely comprised of taxes. The net lifetime contributions of each generation are the total of what they are predicted to contribute in taxes minus what they take out in benefits and public services. The projection assumed that government policies agreed by June 2010 were implemented; that the economy, and therefore per capita tax revenues, grows at an average of two percent per annum; and that real interest rates average at three percent. The population is assumed to continue growing and ageing until 2058, whereafter it stabilises.

The models shows the gap between revenue and expenditure (excluding interest payment on Government debt), expressed as a percentage of GDP, closing from 2008 until 2018 and then increasing to 2058, mainly due to the increases in age-related expenditure with an aging population. The projected net contributions of different generations continues to increase long into the future. The average for those not yet born in 2008 (£159,668) is markedly higher than for those aged 25 (the Millennial generation born 1983) (£124,486), which is much higher in turn compared with those aged 65 (baby boomers born 1945), who make a negative net contribution (−£223,183). According to the model, in order for future generations to receive the same net benefits as those born in 2008, taxes would have had to have risen by 15.4 percent from 2010, and even then the baby boomer generation, with declining tax liabilities, would have done much better than those born in 2008 or after. Given that we now know that taxes did not rise by this amount, and that plans for the elimination of the budget deficit by 2018 have now been abandoned, these projections of ongoing intergenerational inequalities are likely to be conservative.

These are predictions, estimated on the basis of 2010 policies and population projections, and, even if the population estimates prove accurate, policies may, of course, change. However, on the current trends, it does seem highly likely that the Millennials, and the generations coming after, will end up contributing much more to the welfare state than they take out over their lifetimes, whereas the baby boomer generation will take out more than it contributed. Taking account of the generational transfers occurring through housing markets and private pensions, only partially offset by inheritances, this will amount to a very substantial inequity between these generations over the life course. The intergenerational welfare contract will have broken down.

CHAPTER 6

Policies for Intergenerational Equity: (1) Education and Work

Policies for reducing intergenerational and age-related inequality potentially span all the domains discussed in this book. They can be applied in education, work, housing and in relation to welfare costs and benefits. For many people they must reach further still, including into the political domain. Reducing the voting age to 16, for instance, is supported by three of the major political parties in England, including, Labour, the Liberal Democrats and the Greens, with an active campaign in support by the Electoral Reform Society and the Votes at 16 Coalition. Not least important amongst the arguments in favour is that it would help reduce the growing demographic imbalance in electoral politics. To discuss the full range of relevant policies, however, would require a book in itself. In all policy debates the devil is in the detail, and the details cannot be rapidly glossed. This chapter concentrates only on policies for education and transitions to work, and the next on housing. They take housing because this is area where intergenerational inequality is most marked and education because it is amenable, at least in some areas, to some relatively simple policy reforms which would make a difference.

The education systems in the UK are not the primary cause of mounting intergenerational inequality. In fact, as we saw in Chap. 3, education remains one area where young people feel they are better off than their parents were. They have several years longer in school and get higher qualifications than their parents did. We have some of the very best universities in the world, with the system generally performing better than ever in the international league tables, and we punch above our weight in the contribution that HE makes to research and innovation. Britain is still a world leader in innovation, despite the relatively low investment in Research and Development,[1] and this is largely down to the excellence of our university research. The school A level examination system, whatever else its faults, is very effective in preparing young people for more specialised higher education studies. A level graduates have a head start, for instance, against the average high school graduate in the US who starts university education with rather little specialist disciplinary knowledge.

But there is one major problem with the education systems in the UK which has, arguably, got worse for the younger generation. Our systems produce very unequal skills outcomes, and are doing very little, if anything, to improve our comparatively low and stalling levels of social mobility.[2] These failures pertain across the UK, but since Scotland, Wales and Northern Ireland have separate education systems, we concentrate in the policy discussion here on the predominant part—the system in England.

This education system in England has always been highly diverse and fragmented, and many would say it is becoming less like a system all the time. With the relentless promotion since the 1980s of a market-oriented agenda of school choice, diversity and competition, we have regressed in some ways to the educational voluntarism of the 19th century. This prized school diversity and independence above all else, but educational provision in England then lagged well behind what was available in other advanced states in terms of universalism and inclusiveness.[3] Contemporary testimony to English educational backwardness in the 19th century is ample. From the declaration of the Select Committee in 1818 'that England is the worst educated country in Europe', to Balfour's assertion in 1902 that 'England is behind all continental rivals in education', contemporary debates were littered with comparisons with European systems, almost invariably to England's detriment.[4] In terms of inclusiveness in education we are in danger of becoming once again a laggard in European education.

The evidence of our relatively high levels of inequality is very clear from the cross-national data on educational qualifications and skills, considered in Chap. 2. Inequality in educational attainments (in terms of highest qualifications achieved) has reduced over the years but is still higher amongst 25–34 years olds in England than in all but three of the OECD countries in the Survey of Adult Skills (Spain, Italy and Northern Ireland).[5] Inequality in skills opportunities and outcomes is relatively high, though not extreme, at 15 years, according to the results of successive PISA surveys. Inequality of outcomes can be measured by the degree of variation in student scores. The UK ranked 11th out of 34 OECD countries on this measure for literacy in the 2009 PISA survey.[6] Inequality of skills opportunity can be measured by the impact of social background on achievement. On this measure the UK ranked 7th most unequal of the OECD countries.[7] But things seem to get relatively worse during the upper secondary and higher education stages.[8] Most shocking is the level of skills inequality amongst young adults revealed in the SAS. Amongst 25–29 year olds, England has the highest inequality in skills outcomes (measured this time in skills Gini Coefficients) of all countries in the tests for Numeracy and the second highest for Literacy (after the US).[9] On the social gradient measure of inequalities in skills opportunities the story is no better. Amongst 16–24 year olds England ranks 2nd highest in both Numeracy and Literacy on inequality of opportunity (only behind the Slovak Republic).[10] On all of these measures we find greater inequality in skills amongst young people than amongst those aged 55–64. So, unless there are substantial improvements during the life course, which is unlikely, inequalities in skills, unlike in education levels, are getting worse in each generation.

These very high levels of skills inequality matter—for two reasons. Firstly, because skills inequality contributes to wage inequality which is in turn associated with all sorts of negative social consequences.[11] Extreme levels of inequality in earnings and incomes not only represent a major challenge to social cohesion; they are also associated with negative social outcomes across a range of domains, from public health and wellbeing, to social trust, political engagement, social mobility and crime.[12] Skills inequality probably also influences national economic performance, since countries with more unequal skills also tend to have lower average levels of skill and consequently reduced labour productivity.[13] The second reason is that most of the inequality in skills is concentrated at the bottom end of the achievement scale, where the variation across countries is the highest. This takes us back to that third of young people who, as we saw in Chap. 2, fail to complete full upper secondary education and therefore lack a full Level 3 qualification, now considered the minimum across the OECD for successful participation in the labour market. This is the most vulnerable section of our young people and the one that is almost certainly going to fare very much worse in employment over the life course than its equivalents in the parents' generation. So what can be done to improve the performance of the education system with respect to this key group?

The answers with regard to early years learning are perhaps most straightforward. Raising attendance rates in pre-school education is essential to reducing the social gaps in skills which arise early in the lives of children. Most commentators and policy-makers agree on this.[14] Governments balk at the costs of extending entitlements to subsidised pre-school education to children from two years onwards, even though research shows it will probably nearly pay for itself in the longer term by raising the productivity and taxes paid of both mothers and children.[15] Nevertheless, substantial improvements have been made in these areas which will no doubt reduce inequality in skills of older children in the longer term. We just need to take this further, so that subsidies for pre-school education can be extended to two year olds, particularly to those from families on low incomes.

REDUCING INEQUALITY IN LOWER SECONDARY EDUCATION

The biggest challenge lies in what to do with lower secondary schooling where large inequalities stubbornly persist despite the various reforms in the New Labour era to improve the performance of lower achieving children and schools.[16] The relatively high inequalities in secondary schools in the UK can be partly attributed to our high levels of income inequality, which disadvantages poorer families while allowing better-off parents to buy better schooling for their children, either in private schools or by moving to more expensive areas with the better state schools. However, this is not the whole story. OECD cross-country analyses of the PISA data on 15-year olds' skills show only a weak correlation between income inequality and inequality of education opportunity at the country level. In fact, as the OECD report on equity concludes: 'the evidence suggests that, in general, cross-national differences in inequalities of performance are associated more closely with the characteristics of the education system than with underlying social inequalities or measures of economic development.'[17]

The dominant position within current cross-country research on school systems and skills inequality is that more unequal outcomes are likely to occur when there is early selection to differentiated tracks and types of school; a higher proportion of privately funded schools; a lack of standardisation in curricula and assessment; and a federal system where funding is devolved to the regional level.[18] According to this research, early tracking increases inequality as combined peer effects and school effects raise aspirations amongst students in high status tracks and schools and depress aspirations amongst students in lower status tracks and schools.[19] Schools which are entirely privately funded, and have high fees, promote inequality as families with high incomes can buy higher-quality education for their children in schools with smaller class sizes, better resources and better-paid teachers. Lack of standardisation in curricula and assessment systems promotes inequality because school practises become more differentiated according to the social and ability composition of their intakes, thus exacerbating variation in school and peer effects across schools.[20]

The UK suffers from all of these problems. We have a substantial proportion of fully private schools which are, because of their very high fees, almost uniquely elitist amongst systems of private and semi-private schools across the world. We have different education systems in the various nations of the UK which adds to overall UK inequalities. And our school system in England is anything but standardised. While the state school system is notionally non-selective and comprehensive, in practice it is becoming increasingly selective and tracked. Over the past 30 years an obsession with school choice and diversity, and competition between schools, has led to the creation of multiple types of secondary school with different governance and funding, admissions procedures and curriculum priorities. The current list includes free schools, faith schools, studio schools, university technical colleges and academies of various kinds, including sponsored academies, chain academies (ARK, ULT, AET, etc.) and converter academies. Providers include charities, foundations, social enterprises, faith and community groups and private education businesses. These schools are still publicly funded, and controlled, to different degrees, by the state, but the sense of an integrated public system with a public purpose is disappearing. Local Education Authorities have been eviscerated and local planning eroded. Theresa May's plans for a new wave of grammar schools will only add to the problem.

Many of these initiatives have been undertaken in the name of improving standards for children from poorer families in less affluent areas. And there have been some successes, notably recently in standards in London's schools. Improvements here may be partly due to the generally strong and improving performance of the increasing number of children from immigrant families. It may also be in part due to the encouragement of cooperation between schools through initiatives such as New Labour's London Challenge. But across the whole system it is hard to see how educational inequalities can be reduced by a proliferation of different types of school and increasing fragmentation of the school system. Certainly the cross-national evidence does not support this.

There is no evidence that increasing differentiation and competition between schools improves overall standards,[21] although giving schools more autonomy in professional areas (like pedagogy and the curriculum) has been associated with better results in some studies.[22] The education systems in Europe which have most equal educational and skills outcomes, and the smallest social gaps in achievement, are in the Nordic countries. These countries all have private or semi-private school sectors, but the schools are relatively un-elitist because they are state subsidised and charge low fees. The state sectors all operate with non-selective, all-through primary/secondary comprehensive schools. School choice policies have been adopted in some areas, notably in Swedish cities where they have been associated with rising inequality,[23] but overall parents do little school choosing. There are various reasons for this: sparsely populated rural areas offer little choice of schools; all-through schools discourage changes of school at the end of the primary phase; and schools tend to be very similar anyway. The key to the relatively low inequality in Nordic systems lies in the low differentiation between schools. Schools tend to be similar both in the social balance of their intakes and in their average performance levels.[24] The two are connected.

In most countries the educational achievement of children is influenced less by their social background than by the nature of the school they attend and the children they go to school with. OECD analyses show that over one third of all the variation in individual student performance in PISA tests across the OECD can be attributed to differences in average school performance, and the school characteristic which most influences school performance is the nature of its intake.[25] Based on PISA 2006 data, OECD calculates that in most OECD countries the social intake of the school 'far outweighs the effects of the individual students' socio-economic background' on student scores.[26] The social composition of the school has such a large impact because it affects everything else about the school, including what are referred to as 'peer effects' and 'school effects'—meaning the impact of other children and of the school ethos. Across all the OECD countries, the social intake of the school (measured by the educational and occupational level of parents) explains about 55 percent of the difference in average performance between schools. However, in some countries, including in Luxembourg, the UK, the US and New Zealand, the proportion is much higher, in the UK case 77 percent. This compares within 23 percent in Finland and 26 percent in Norway.

Educational and skills outcomes in England are very unequal, in part because schools vary so much in the social mix of their intakes, which are much more differentiated than in Scotland, for instance.[27] Intake differences exacerbate differences in school norms and drive up inequalities in outcomes. But how do you change this? Nordic countries, except perhaps Sweden, are fairly homogeneous societies with relatively low levels of inequality. But England's populations, particularly in the large cities, are extremely diverse and income inequality is higher. How can the school system be designed so that it creates less inequality in this context? A number of structural changes are theoretically possible.

We could roll back the diversity and choice agenda, which has so far produced no evidence of raising average levels of achievement or reducing inequality. According to the OECD's commentary on England's performance in the latest (2015) PISA survey, standards, at least in English, Maths and Science, have flat-lined for a decade. This would mean reversing the proliferation of school types and abolishing the myriad distinctions between faith schools, academics, local authority community schools and so on. Local authorities could be given back responsibility for school admissions and instructed to reduce inequalities in school intakes by introducing the 'banding' system which, under the former Inner London Education Authority, required each school to have a balance of pupils of different levels of prior achievement. School catchment areas could also be re-introduced across the board, with local authorities being required to review and, if necessary, redraw their boundaries regularly. Denmark already operates such a system. This would help to avoid the post-code lottery which allows residential segregation by social class and ethnicity to skew school intakes and concentrate a disproportionate number of minority ethnic and second language speaking children in particular schools. Recent research by Demos, for instance, shows that 50 percent of non-white students are in schools where minority ethnic students are in a majority. As the Government commissioned Casey Review points out, this cannot be good for integration and social cohesion.[28]

Other measures could be adopted which have been seen to work in other European and Asian countries. School heads and teachers could be rotated between schools, as happens in Japan, to equalise resource distribution between schools.[29] Private schools could be integrated into the state sector, either as 11–18 schools or as Sixth Form Colleges, as in most European countries: given sufficient autonomy to provide pedagogically and confessionally distinctive forms of education for those who want it, but with low, state-subsidised fees to make them accessible to a wider range of students. Distinctive school specialisms in state schools could be maintained, but admissions policies would not allow school specialisms to justify selection in admissions based on academic achievement.

More radical still would be to abolish the outdated distinction between secondary schools with and without sixth forms, since this represents one of the biggest divides between secondary schools. Traditionally, the sixth form has been regarded a key marker of a good secondary school and schools without one are often seen as second class. Current Government policy is that all new academies should have sixth forms, so we are moving in he direction of giving all schools sixth forms. However, the school sixth form is often an expensive and ineffective way of providing universal upper secondary education. School sixth forms are rarely big enough to sustain a wide range of subjects so they often neglect the creative arts, technical subjects and less popular foreign languages. They tend to focus on a narrow range of academic subjects that do not appeal to all young people.

Sixth-form and tertiary colleges, on the other hand, have been highly successful and very popular. Their A level results are on average ten percent better than those of sixth forms in state secondary schools, and their students are more likely to progress to Russell Group universities and universities generally.[30] Many young people prefer to progress at 16 to a new institution with a more adult environment. Unfortunately, there are currently only 93 of them country-wide and only one in five teenagers live within five miles of one. Sixth-Form Colleges feel under threat because of the forward march of academies with sixth forms. Many parents with children in schools with sixth forms defend them vigorously, but that is partly due to the lack of good alternatives in their area. Much more rational and efficient than proliferating new academies with small sixth forms would be to introduce—gradually—an institutional break at 15/16, as in most other European and East Asian countries. We should create a dedicated upper secondary system of sixth-form colleges and FE colleges. Sixth-form colleges would provide the comprehensive academic and technical curriculum for 16–18 year olds in every area. FE colleges should be rationalised and more centralised, providing the full range of 16–18 provision but focusing more on the specialised technical areas which relate to local industries and which require expensive equipment to deliver the curriculum.

All of these changes would be administratively possible, although not necessarily popular in schools which have seen incessant short-term reforms over a period of 30 years. Much would need to be done to keep teachers and heads on board, even though many might in principle agree with the aims. Restoring New Labour's successful school renovation programme, *Building Schools for the Future*, which was controversially scrapped by the former Coalition Government's Education Secretary, Michael Gove, would no doubt provide a useful tonic. A concerted effort to restore the status of teaching as a profession would also help. The main challenge, though, would be to develop a political vision for education which prioritised the equalisation of opportunities and out-comes, and which brought parents together to support the means to do this. After many years of policy moving in the opposite direction this would not be easy.

Reforming Upper Secondary Education and Training

Reforming upper secondary education and training may be easier than changing lower secondary education because just about everyone agrees it is failing, most notably because of the absence of a strong vocational provision within it. The system has an absurdly complex structure of pro-viders, courses and qualifications. This confuses young people, parents and employers, and deprives this phase of education of the normative standards which are essential for encouraging achievement and reduc-ing inequality. We not only have sixth-forms, in all the various types of secondary school; we also have Sixth-Form Colleges, Tertiary Colleges, Further Education Colleges, and an army of private training provid-ers, some charitable and not-for-profit foundations and other for-profit. The recent Sainsbury Review was not able to say how many of these there are, but noted that they account for 30 percent of the adult skills budget.[31] Courses on offer vary hugely in duration, standard and quality and there is no common core of learning across all the different courses and programmes.

In the absence of a proper national qualification system, England—uniquely amongst nations—operates a market in educational qualifications. This has produced a dense jungle of awards which no-one understands, least of all the students or the employers who use them for recruitment. In 2015 there were officially over 21,000 vocational qualifications on Ofqual's Register of Regulated Qualifications, excluding GCSEs and A levels. These were offered by 158 different awarding organisations. Of these awards over 12,000 were eligible for public funding for teaching to 16–18 year olds. An individual aiming for a future in plumbing, for example, could choose between 33 qualifications offered at three different levels by five different awarding organisations.[32] Because of the Byzantine complexity of this under-regulated vocational market in providers, programmes and qualifications, there is an overall lack of transparency in the sector which undermines its credibility and value. The programmes on offer vary too much in content and quality and many of the qualifications awarded are worthless on the labour market, as we saw in Chap. 2.

The over-arching aim of any systemic reform to our upper secondary education must be to create a set of academic and vocational pathways for young people that are all comprehensible and valued; which have transparent standards and which lead to more predictable destinations in the labour market or to higher levels of education and training. A break at 15/16, with a new and simplified institutional structure with dedicated upper secondary institutions would be the most rational way of organising the system, but might not be essential. The main point would be to reduce and clarify the pathways and qualifications, so that there was greater standardisation with regard to the duration, content and quality of the different programmes on offer. A strong argument can be made in favour of a normative three-year duration for upper secondary programmes, to bring students up to the standard in other countries which mostly have three-year upper secondary programmes. A common core of Maths and English—and possibly Civics—with structured work placements on vocational courses, should be mandatory for all programmes. The Sainsbury Review goes some way in this direction, although it sticks with the two-year programme as the norm. The Governments' Green Paper on industrial strategy[33] floats the idea of a new Transition Year at school for lower achieving students, but this would be demoralising for those at the end of lower secondary school and it would be better to incorporate the additional year into upper-secondary education.

The Review recommends a set of 15 main technical pathways at the upper secondary level, with a nod towards the Scandinavian countries which have a similar arrangement. The organising principle behind the pathways is the notion of the skilled occupation, broadly defined, as in the German concept of the *Beruf*. The Review rightly argues that technical education should be occupationally-based since this is what provides its value on the labour market. That means avoiding the weakness of previous arrangements whereby vocational qualifications were either too general to serve as a preparation for entry to jobs, as with the now defunct General National Vocational Qualifications, or too job- and firm-specific, as with many NVQs, to serve as initial occupational training for young people. Confusingly, the Review still organises the technical programmes around sectors, rather than occupations existing across sectors. Nevertheless, within each sectorally-defined pathway there would be options which would be increasingly specific to occupations and occupational clusters as students progressed through their programmes. These occupational designations would appear on certificates awarded, along with details of work placements completed, and this would give employers a clearer idea of what the award holder could do.

Technical pathways in upper secondary education need to be offered in both work-based modes and college-based modes, but these need to be integrated within a single system. Britain will never create the encompassing set of high quality Dual System apprenticeships taken by upwards of 40 percent of young people in countries like Austria, Germany and Switzerland. We had such a system for ten years or so after the 1964 Industrial Training Act, but the social partnership and sectoral infrastructure on which it was based has now been demolished and can't easily be re-created. Nevertheless, apprenticeships can still have a place in upper secondary provision if organised on the hybrid model, as adopted in countries like Denmark, Netherlands and Singapore, where the state plays the coordinating role, and where employment-based apprenticeships are combined with college-based apprenticeships. Even countries like Germany are having to adopt a similar plurality of modes now with the shortfall in employer-offered apprentice contracts.

Our current apprenticeships are moving in this direction but their design is still full of flaws. Some are very good, but many are too short and most do not lead beyond Level 2 qualifications. This defeats the whole objective of the apprenticeship which is to prepare young people for skilled work at craft and technician levels (for which they need to be qualified at Level 3 or Level 4). Absurdly, most apprenticeships now are taken by those already employed who are over 19 years of age. The situation has occurred because the regulations allow it, and because employers take advantage of the Government subsidies to place existing employees, who already have many of the skills to gain qualifications, on apprentice contracts. A mere six percent of 16–18 year olds are currently taking apprenticeships.[34] This situation has to change. Apprenticeships should be primarily for young people and must lead toward skilled craft and technician level qualifications. New government measures to specify minimum levels of off-the-job training and duration of programmes, and to require attainment of prescribed standards in English and Maths, are moving in the right direction, but much more needs to be done to make the system credible and fit for purpose.

Because apprenticeships are never likely to provide the main pathway for technical education for young people we need an alternative of high quality, college-based technical provision. The pathways, as advocated by the Sainsbury Review, should be aligned with the apprenticeship, sharing skills standards and a common core curriculum, and leading to the same overarching qualifications, just as occurs in France with the CAP qualifications taken by both apprentices in centres d'apprentissage and by vocational students in the Lycée Professionnel. Their delivery modes, however, would be different. Instead of the on-the-job learning enjoyed by apprentices, college-based technical students would need to undertake structured work placements. The Sainsbury Review recommends that the placements should be prepared in advance and monitored by their college lecturers. Students would keep a log of their activities and what they had learned, and employers would provide a report, both of which necessary for successful completion. Colleges would receive additional funds of around £500 for each placement. A new system of national technical awards would be developed under the aegis of the new Institute for Apprenticeship which would convene expert panels to determine the skills standards relevant for each occupational branch of each award. All of this makes a lot of sense. However, in crucial respects it does not go far enough.

Firstly, work placements are envisaged to last for about four to six weeks. This is far too short for the work placement to be a credible substitute for the on-the-job experience of the apprentice. In France the equivalent would be the 'stage' which typically lasts six months or more. The objection to longer placements would be the difficulty of finding employers to provide them. Indeed our FE colleges, which in recent years have lost many of their networks with local employers, might find this difficult. But a rationalisation of college provision, currently underway with the so called Area Reviews, might make this feasible again. Colleges should be encouraged to re-develop their sectoral specialisms, which foster the close links with local employers that would make extended work placements for technical students more feasible. Whether the Government needs to set up yet another kind of institution—like the Institutes of Technology proposed in the Green Paper—needs more thought. Re-purposing further education colleges, many of which are excellent, might be more effective.

Secondly, the proposed new state-led system of technical qualifications still falls short of the full national system it aspires to. The Institute of Apprenticeship and Technical Education—a proposed Government agency which would develop occupational standards and have oversight over the qualification system—is comprised of 'experts' working in an independent capacity; college organisations, trades unions and professional associations are not represented as of right, although they may be called upon. There is no mention of the volume of labour market research that might be needed to develop these standards. This is a German-style BIBB lite. The BIBB (Federal Institute for Vocational Education and Training) in Germany, which develops the skills standards for occupational qualifications, employs some 600 people, many of them researchers. Representatives of employers, trade unions, Germany's federal states and the federal government work together on the BIBB Board. The institutional set-up recognizes that developing occupational standards is a complicated business in which many different parties have legitimate interests. The proposed slim-line Institute of Apprenticeship cannot conceivably perform the same function itself.

Instead, the Sainsbury Review recommends that it puts contracts for developing occupational standards out to tender. In a similar way, private awarding bodies will be invited to become sole providers of awards in each technical area. But it will still be private bodies who will be awarding 'national' certificates. And this will not solve the problem of standards being eroded by private awarding bodies offering 'easier' qualifications to increase their market share. In this case they will just be competing for market share with different awarding bodies offering qualifications in other technical areas, rather than alternative qualifications for the same occupation. The Review makes a strong case for putting the state in charge of national qualifications, but then in practice brings the market back in to develop and award qualifications.

The ambivalence about state and market runs through the report. There is the constant and familiar refrain about an 'employer-led system'. Then follows a powerful advocacy of state responsibility for the overall qualification system. This is a misconceived dualism. If they are to be coherent and credible, national qualifications need be awarded by the state, not by private bodies. Employers, professional associations and trades unions all need to be centrally involved in the process, but their various views and interests should be concerted through a representative body convened by the state.

While moving in the right direction, the recommendations for achieving higher standards of literacy and numeracy amongst vocational students lack bite. Requiring students on technical courses to reach a specified minimum standard in Maths and English to achieve their certificates, as is now the case on apprenticeships, is essential, and has been standard practice in most countries. How this will be achieved is barely discussed and colleges are to be left to decide how to organise the learning in these areas. The learning of English and Maths should be geared towards requirements of the technical subjects of the programmes in question. This already happens in colleges. The problem is how to raise the profile of these areas of the vocational curriculum. Establishing dedicated curriculum areas, and indeed even dedicated classes with specified minimum hours, is one possibility. But the bigger issue is how to raise the standard of teaching. Much of the English and Maths teaching in colleges is undertaken by lecturers who are not specialists in the subjects and who have not been trained to teach them. Driving up the standards in these core subjects would require giving them much more prominence in the curriculum and also hiring many more specialist lecturers. Class contact hours on vocational courses also need to be reviewed. At present, vocational students in colleges often have far fewer hours in the classroom or workshop than the typical A level student in a sixth-form college. French Level 3 vocational students typically spend 30–36 hours per week in the classroom or workshop, on courses that last three years. In England vocational students often have only half this level of teacher contact and their courses are shorter. If we want our vocational students to reach the standards achieved in other countries, we will have to invest much more in giving them the time to do so.

TERTIARY EDUCATION

Tertiary education in England also needs some major reforms. We have succeeded in raising participation in university higher education to near 50 percent, which is a considerable achievement. But arguably too many are now going into general university higher education while too few take higher-level technical tertiary courses. The supply of university-trained graduates is beginning to outstrip demand for graduate skills in the labour market and the returns to bachelors degrees are likely to decline, if they have not already done so. The wage premium for graduates has held up in most countries—graduates are still likely over their lifetimes to have higher employment rates and to earn more than non-graduates in most countries. Nevertheless, graduate pay in real terms is declining in many countries and the wage premium is either reducing or becoming more diversified by course and university.[35] Increasing yet further the proportion studying general university degrees, as the Government plans to do with its lifting of the cap on university undergraduate numbers, will only the increase the number of young people graduating with high levels of debt but little chance of finding graduate jobs. They will feel cheated by a system that has promised them high rewards for investing so much in university education but fails to deliver in terms of jobs. This is already happening in the US, where there is rising discontent amongst graduates who have paid high fees to attend less prestigious private universities whose degrees, they discover, are not worth much. Despite this, young people in England still increasingly apply for university higher education courses, despite the debts they will accumulate and the uncertain prospects they will face. But this is partly because there are no good alternatives to university-based tertiary education.

Technical tertiary education, which once flourished in our FE colleges and the former polytechnics, has virtually collapsed. The Higher National Diploma (HND) and Higher National Certificate (HNC) used to be highly regarded technician-level qualifications. Many young people and employed adults studied for them in colleges and polytechnics, either full- or part-time, and they provided an important avenue for career progression, allowing former apprentices and skilled workers advancement into technical, supervisory and management roles. Yet in 2014/2015 only just over 33,000 were enrolled for these courses, mostly in colleges, and the overwhelming majority in Business Studies.

No more than 2.5 percent of university undergraduates were enrolled. Foundation Degrees, a more recent innovation in shorter vocational tertiary provision, dating from 2000, initially did well, recruiting over 80,000 students by 2008/2009.[36] However, the numbers participating declined sharply after the caps on undergraduate numbers were relaxed by Government, with only just over two percent of HE undergraduates now taking these courses. The two main vocational alternatives to 3-year bachelor degrees now enrol just 3.7 percent of undergraduates in HE.

The atrophy of technical tertiary education means the loss of an important avenue for mobility for young people in England. In many of the world's richer countries technical tertiary education is well established and delivers good labour market prospects for young people. OECD analysis of data from 2011 shows that men in OECD countries with short-cycle vocational tertiary education earn on average 26 percent more than those with only upper secondary education, and women 32 percent more. The average return is lower than for Type A higher education, but not by much, and it may be considerably higher for those with lower levels of tertiary attainment and skills. A number of countries have well attended and highly respected technical tertiary education routes, either based in Universities or in other dedicated vocational tertiary institutions. Germany has its technical universities (Facchoschulen) which specialise in applied science and technical degrees, all at the bachelor level, as well as other institutions offering shorter tertiary vocational provision. The Netherlands, likewise, has polytechnics and higher vocational schools offering vocational tertiary provision at various levels. France has over 100 IUTs (Instituts Universitaires de Technologie) which are based in universities and offer two-year degrees in technical subjects. Singapore has developed a large polytechnic sector which enrols over 40 percent of young people on three-year programmes leading to technical qualifications equivalent to the UK's Higher National Diplomas. Interestingly, in this case, the polytechnics recruit young people straight from lower secondary schools, fast-tracking them to short-cycle degree standards by the age of 19 (or older if their studies are interrupted by national service). In all these countries, degrees from these sectors are generally well esteemed and offer good labour market destinations.

So why has this type of provision declined so rapidly in the UK? Part of the answer lies in the fact that we have removed the cap on student numbers on bachelors programmes in HE. Universities have the opportunity to recruit as many as they can onto the high-fee-charging bachelors courses. Prospective students have been led to believe that bachelors degrees offer the best labour market prospects and they tend to chose this option in favour of shorter and less expensive short-cycle degrees despite the higher costs, because their student loans cover the fees which need not be re-paid until later. The perceived prestige attached to the bachelor's degree seems to outweigh the benefits of the lower student debt which would result from taking a shorter degree. This cannot be the whole of the answer, however, because short-cycle technical tertiary education was not that popular even before loans were introduced and caps removed. The fact is that we have not invested enough in technical tertiary education and have not made it attractive enough to prospective students.

A large and effective tertiary sector was created by Singapore's Government from the 1980s, as that country was upgrading its economy from one based on low-cost assembly to advanced, high skills manufacturing.[37] High enrolments were achieved in the polytechnics partly as a result of the stringent limits placed on university admissions. In the early days only a quarter of the school-leaving cohort was allowed attend university. However, the Government also invested massively in the new polytechnic sector, building five new state-of-the-art polytechnic campuses. The new polytechnics boasted exceptionally high quality buildings and learning environments, with extensive IT-based learning, fully computerised lecture theatres, and advanced facilities and equipment for learning manufacturing skills. The latter included fully automated small manufacturing plants with robotic CNC machines and automatic conveyancing. You won't find many FE colleges in England with similar facilities, even now.[38]

Britain needs to re-balance its tertiary education provision if we are to avoid producing a surplus of graduates with high levels of debt and poor employment prospects. Creating an attractive range of short-cycle technical degrees in colleges and universities would make an important contribution to this. To achieve this we need to restore the caps of student numbers in bachelors programmes and invest more in developing the curricula and facilities for these technical programmes. We also need to change the funding incentives so that universities and colleges invest in high quality short-cycle degrees.

Policy-makers also need to look again at the conditions in the labour market for students and young graduates. In many ways young employees and job-seekers are at the sharp of globalisation. Because they are new to the labour market, and the least protected by tenure and unions, they are the first to experience any new employment trend that seeks to increase 'labour flexibility' as a way for employers to reduce operating costs. The latest manifestations of this are the proliferation of unpaid internships and 'zero-hours' contracts. Both are currently on a sharp upward curve. Zero-hours contracts are becoming endemic to the so-called gig-economy, but also elsewhere. Uber and Deliveroo are just the tip of the iceberg.

Firms favour so-called the zero-hours contracts because it allows them maximum flexibility—and therefore lower costs—in deploying labour. Increasingly they are engaging people to provide services on an ostensibly 'self-employed basis' so that they can get away with minimum hourly rates and avoid paying national insurance contributions and holiday pay. But, as tribunals and courts are now beginning to acknowledge, their workers are in reality employees. They are bound to accept whatever tasks their employers give them, have little discretion over how to perform them, and are frequently denied the right to work for another employer.

Unpaid internships are also becoming an increasingly common means for exploiting young people. Periods of unpaid work experience, as part of organised study programmes, or undertaken privately for short periods to gain a sense of working life in a particularly industry, are legitimate. The employers gain little in productive output. But internships which are not part of study programmes, or which are undertaken privately, but exceed a month in duration, should count as employment and be subject to employment law and living wage legislation. In both cases, with zero-hours contracts and internships, employer evasion of standard employment rights should be stopped.

STUDENT FINANCE

Lastly, there is the vexed question of student finance. The current system of fees and loans is unsupportable and is heading for a big crash. It's morally indefensible because it is encouraging a whole generation of young people to acquire huge debts which they will be paying off through much of their adult lives while also paying historically high proportions of their incomes on rent or mortgages. And it is highly inequitable for two reasons. Firstly, because one generation is paying for a service which previous generations have had for free. And secondly, because tuition fees are much the same for all courses. Once over the earnings threshold of £21,000 pa, and until loans are written off 30 years later, graduates pay back the full loan plus interest for fees which were virtually the same for each course, irrespective of what it is worth on the labour market. The income level at which they start to repay can be changed by Government and is now being lowered.

The other problem with the system is that it has proved to be very expensive and promises to get more so. The Institute for Fiscal Studies (IFS) estimate that, given the proportion of graduates not earning enough to pay back their loans in full, taxpayers will end up paying 43 percent of the value of loans.[39] With rises in tuition charges resulting from the removal of fee caps, and including other Government support packages for teacher training and broadening access to higher education, the long-run public costs of the current system would be £24,592 per full-time student and £7.4 bn in total per year for full-time students in England.[40]

The current mess in the financing higher education could have been avoided. There was always a simpler and more equitable solution available in the form of an all-age graduate tax. This could be designed as an additional income tax of, say, 2.5 percent, levied on all English-domiciled graduates who received subsidised undergraduate education in English universities and are earning above £21,000 pa (the current loan repayment threshold). Neither of the reports on higher education finance by Dearing and Browne[41] gave serious thought to a graduate tax. UK university leaders were always against it, because it meant relying on governments for most of their funding. They preferred to have the money direct from fees (which in time they could regulate). Nor would the scheme have been popular amongst graduates who had benefitted from tuition-free higher education. But the efficiency and equity arguments for such a tax are unimpeachable.

The tax would be simple to levy through the HMRC self-assessment system. A small number of graduates might avoid it for periods by working abroad, but the number of these would be much lower than the proportion in the current system who will not pay back their loans. The tax would meet the government's own principle that students should contribute substantially towards the cost of a higher education from which they have benefitted financially. And it would be much fairer than the current system. Graduates would pay back in proportion to their earnings which derive, at least in part, from the value of the particular courses they had taken and the degrees they had acquired. A small extra tax on graduate earnings could raise a substantial part of the annual costs of first degree higher education.

Grant is based on income of parents - not fair

Some rough estimates of the sums involved in England suggest the feasibility of such a system. In 2016 there were some 6.3 million English-domiciled graduates, aged 20 to 64 and in employment, who were likely to have received subsidised first degree education in England, having been born in England or elsewhere in the EEA and arriving in England before the age of 21. Of these, 74 percent were earning over £21,000 pa, with mean earnings in this group of £43,500 and taxable pay of £32,500.[42]   An all-age graduate tax of 2.5 percent on this group would currently yield an average annual graduate tax payment of £812 per person and just under £3.8bn in total annual tax revenue. The total cost in English universities of full- and part-time first degree undergraduate study for students domiciled in England or born in non-UK EU countries—including university costs and maintenance costs—can be estimated to be £11.8 bn.[43] The all-age graduate tax would cover around 32 percent of these total costs, with a taxpayer annual subsidy of around £8 bn.

The annual public cost of this system would be comparable to that of the current system of fees and loans. The IFS estimate that the taxpayer subsidies for undergraduate education for full-time students in England—including loan subsidies, teaching grants and maintenance grants—was £7.4 bn pa (at 2014 prices). We can estimate that at 2016 prices, and including part-time students, the public costs in 2016 were over £8.25 bn pa, somewhat above that under the proposed graduate tax.[44] An additional boost to the 2015 level of maintenance grants, raising the maximum to, say, £5,000 pa, would bring the public subsidy under a graduate tax to a similar level as the current subsidy.[45]

Writing off student loans, and replacing them with a graduate tax and enhanced maintenance grants, leaves the current taxpayer subsidy for undergraduate education largely unchanged. However, it represents an immediate additional revenue for the Government which is currently paying the full cost of tuition fees by funding the loans issued by the Student Loan Company and which will not see the loans repaid for many years. Over the longer term, all-age graduate taxes will also generate increasing annual tax revenue. Even assuming that HE participation rates soon peak, the proportion of graduates in the labour force will continue rising until 2067 when the current cohort of 18 year olds—with 48 percent participation rates in HE—reach retirement age. By this time nearly half the labour force will be graduates and, even allowing for some decline in the graduate employment rate, there would be some 50 percent more graduate employees liable for the graduate tax than in 2017, with a proportionate increase in the revenue from the tax.

Over the long term the public subsidy required when financing higher education through an all-age graduate tax should be lower than that through loans. However, the greatest advantage of this system is that the tax payments would impact far less on the current generation of graduates than loan repayments do, particularly between the ages of 25 and 50 when financial burdens are highest. Under the current system graduates earning over £21,000 pay back their loans at nine percent of their earnings over £21,000 until their remaining loans are written off 30 years later. For those on average earnings for this group this amounts to repayments of £2,025 pa, compared with the £812 pa that would be paid in graduate tax.

Typical graduate annual repayments under the current loan system are two to three times higher than they would be under a graduate tax and the gap will grow as the caps on fees are lifted and average tuition fees rise. Under the proposed graduate tax, governments would be likely to resist paying higher tuition subsidies to universities, and graduate contributions through the graduate tax would remain stable in real terms. Direct public funding of higher education for undergraduates would also avoid the growth in inequality in access to high quality undergraduate courses which would arise with the increasing differentiation of fees resulting from the lifting of the fee caps.

It would have been difficult to win political support for such a tax ten years ago, before fees and loans had been introduced. Now that we know all the negative consequences of those reforms, not least to current and future generations of young people starting life with huge debts, the graduate tax might be considered in more favourable terms. The case should certainly be argued. There are few measures that would more visibly improve intergenerational equity.

CHAPTER 7

Policies for Intergenerational Equity Two: Housing

The only response to Britain's housing crisis on which nearly everyone is agreed, at least in principle, is on the need to increase the supply of homes. On most estimates, we need to build some 250,000–300,000 new homes a year to keep pace with the rising demand for housing units.[1] This would restore home building to its historic levels in the 30 years after World War Two, trebling the rate of new building in recent years. The questions are: what is holding back building now; what kind of homes do we need and where; and who should be building them.

The Government blames the low rate of building on restrictive local planning regulations, the slow 'build-out' of sites with planning permission and the lack of competition amongst the major building companies. Its latest White Paper, *Fixing our Broken Housing Market*,[2] aims to boost construction through a new £3 bn fund for small building firms, relaxation of local planning regulations, and by putting additional pressure on local authorities and neighbourhoods to draw up ambitious new plans for development. They are relying primarily on incentives to private developers to double their current rate of building. However, private developers are never going to deliver enough new homes at affordable prices. It is in their interest to hoard land, keep supply restricted and prices high. They will certainly not deliver on the Government's 2015 Manifesto promise—missing in the White Paper—to deliver 225,000 new 'affordable homes' in this Parliament.

In recent years the record of governments in delivering homes at affordable prices has been dismal. According to government figures,

© The Author(s) 2017
A. Green, *The Crisis for Young People*,
DOI 10.1007/978-3-319-58547-5_7

only 32,110 'affordable homes' were built in 2015[3] which was less than in any year since 1991. The White Paper proposals will not change this. In fact the measures proposed are derisory and much weaker even than what we had before. The requirement used to be that new developments had to include at least 20 percent of homes at affordable prices. The White Paper's provisions for 'Starter Homes' now includes just a 'policy *expectation* that housing sites deliver a minimum of ten percent affordable housing.' Unacknowledged in the White Paper is that the Government has recently diluted its definition of 'affordable.' This now means at 80 percent of market value. With the average market price for a starter home in the UK now at around £211,000, an 'affordable' starter home costs 7.4 times the average earnings of 25–29 year olds, some three times the ratio that applied in the 1970s and 80s.[4]

The only way Britain is going to build enough affordable homes to rent or buy is to increase the supply of social housing through empowering housing associations and local authorities to build more. We know this can be done through a mixture of private development and state-led building initiatives. In the 1960s, between 300,000 and 400,000 new homes were built each year, almost half of these by local councils. It was only after the introduction of Right to Buy policies in the 1980s, and the limits then placed on councils replacing the homes they sold, that councils have built fewer and fewer homes. They are still not allowed to use all the receipts from the high quality homes they are obliged to sell for building new homes, and they are subject to an overall cap on borrowing for home building. It is not therefore surprising that they built only 2080 homes in the 12 months to June 2016.

Yet it is the local authorities which are best placed to build affordable homes where they are needed. They often have better access to land, particularly that held in the public sector, than private developers; they could be given powers of compulsory purchase where developers fail to build on land with planning permission; and they know what local communities need. Furthermore, they have access to cheaper borrowing than private developers and they don't have to price in the 25 percent profit margins that most large developers expect. They can therefore price homes for rent or sale more reasonably. Some councils, like in Birmingham and Hackney, have already started ambitious new development programmes, often mixing affordable homes to buy and rent on the same sites. More than a third of UK local authorities are now setting up their own housebuilding companies.⁵ They are only being held back by the fixation of governments on market solutions to the housing problem.

A mixed private and public sector response to Britain's housing crisis is the only one which is going to work. So it is necessary to invest substantial public funds in the process. Governments will have to lift the borrowing caps on local authorities even if this adds to the overall figure for public debt. And they will have to subsidise local authority building programmes if we are to alleviate our chronic housing crisis. To those who say public funding of house building on this scale is not affordable, there is a simple answer. It is a much better use of tax payers' money than the current alternative. This involves public spending of over £27 billion per annum on housing benefits to help low-income tenants pay their rents—money which often ends up in the pockets of private landlords, many of whom provide a very poor service.

Capital Gains Tax on Sales of First Homes

However, increasing the supply of homes will never in itself solve the problems in housing. Too many of the new homes will start—or end up—commanding high prices in the private sector, and too many of them will be bought by buy-to-let landlords and foreign investors rather than would-be home owners. We already have more rooms per person than ever, a surplus of homes to households, and an estimated 600,000 homes left vacant across the country. The problem is that too many of our homes are in the wrong places, at the wrong prices, and they are being bought by the wrong people. Reducing the current gross inequities, generational and otherwise, in home ownership and housing tenures generally requires a more radical approach which reduces incentives for speculation in property and restores the notion that homes exist to meet people's rights for safe and secure places to live. This means going back to basic economic incentives.

House prices have risen so high in many areas of England mainly because property is seen as an exceptionally lucrative investment. This is not a natural characteristic of housing—bricks and mortar don't have any magic property for yielding profit—and in many countries property is not regarded as a particularly good investment. That it has become so in Britain is largely because governments over many decades have systematically favoured property ownership, either because they wished to promote the benefits of a 'property-owning democracy' or, less admirably, because they just wished to keep the majoritarian property-owning electorate onside. The most flagrant case of this has been the tax privileges conferred on home owners and landlords. Historically these privileges included tax deductible mortgage interest for ordinary home owners. Until very recently, they still included special tax privileges for landlords who could set their mortgage interest, plus maintenance and insurance costs, against rental profits for tax purposes.

However, much the most egregious example of tax privilege for property ownership has been the exemption of so called 'first homes' from the capital gains taxes which are paid on profits from the sale of most other assets worth more than £6000. If you invest in paintings or jewelry or other valuable assets you have to pay tax on the profit you make when you sell them. But not in the case of 'first homes'. In the days when most home-buyers were seeking, first and foremost, a place to live for their family, and when house values were not rising so fast, CTG exemption may have made some sense. However, few would claim today that asset maximisation was absent from their considerations when buying a house. Making a good investment is at the heart of people's decisions to buy homes to live in. It has to be—it is the biggest investment most people ever make. For small-time buy-to-let landlords it is the key to their exceptional profits, and they too benefit from CGT exemptions through the simple trick of re-designating supplementary homes as first homes prior to sale.

Tax exemption on capital gains from housing transactions is both socially and fiscally indefensible. It is socially indefensible because it represents the state providing economic favours to one section of the community (older home owners) at the expense of another (younger would-be home buyers). The latter, as a result of the tax incentives for property investment, have to pay higher prices to older vendors. It is fiscally indefensible because it skews investment too much into one unproductive and already bloated sector, and away from other sectors which are more productive, like manufacturing. Rather few people invest in shares in public companies—despite all the hype about the share-owning society—but half the population invests most of their money in property.

No-one any longer seriously tries to defend tax privileges for property on the grounds of principles, either social or economic. The argument about home-owner democracy looks increasingly feeble when the phenomenon is literally disappearing before our eyes. The claim that state support for property ownership is necessary because it boosts the financial sectors on which national economic growth depends is dubious at best, the more so now since it was housing finance which detonated the global financial crash in 2007/2008. Indeed the only remaining justification you hear for tax privileges for property ownership are ones of political expediency and misplaced short-term economic pragmatism. Governments will not consider reforming fiscal policy on property because they think it will be unpopular with older home-owners. They fear any interventions which bring down property prices will tank the economy. Both arguments are short-term in the extreme.

Soaring property prices and associated levels of mortgage debt have already crashed the economy once and will no doubt do so again if things are left to go on as they are. Raising any taxes is certainly unpopular and introducing a new tax (CTG on first homes) would initially be unpopular with a lot of people, it is true. But with the ever rising public debt some increases in taxation are now seen are as inevitable by many economists. The question will be which kinds of tax increases will be most efficient economically and will best meet the social objectives to which people most aspire. With increasing concerns about intergenerational inequity and about the adverse social consequences of rising inequalities in incomes and wealth, it is not impossible to conceive of winning electoral majorities in favour of raising revenues through higher taxation of property assets in exchange for smaller increases in income or other taxes. It should at least be debated.

Collecting taxes on property is relatively straightforward. Immobile physical assets are harder to conceal than less visible financial assets and other more mobile physical assets and their taxation is harder to avoid. Imposing CGT on sales of all homes would also raise considerable revenue. During the seven years preceding the financial crisis in 2008 some 15 million home-owners, who were owner-occupiers throughout the decade, saw the value of their collective housing assets grow by about £1.5 trillion.[6] Netting out for inflation and home improvements, you can estimate real private asset gains of over one trillion pounds. Roughly one million private residential homes were sold each year in the period after 2010.[7] If capital gains tax had been applied over the following five years at 30 percent on annual sales of, say, three million homes owned since the year 2000, with an average net profit of £100,000 and upwards, it would have raised over £90 billion pounds. Tax on the sale of another two million homes, owned over a shorter duration and only netting an average of, say, £50,000 profit, would have been a further £30 billion.

Around £24 billion would have been raised for the Exchequer each year. This is close to what the Government currently spends on secondary education.

Introducing CGT on all property sales, if managed properly, would bring down house prices permanently and this would be a good thing, not just for would-be buyers, but ultimately for everybody, since a more stable housing market would also mean a more stable economy generally. Home owners of long standing who sold their homes would indeed have to pay back in tax some of the windfall paper profits they had made from rising house prices. Forfeited profits would be less for those who had not owned their current properties for so long and for future generations of owners who would see less profit anyway. Most home owners have less to lose from falling house prices than they often imagine. If they sell and re-purchase, they will be selling at lower prices but also buying more cheaply. If they stay put, their housing assets may have declined on paper, but so long as they can pay the mortgage they still have a roof over their heads—in a property they have chosen to buy.

Hardest hit would be those who had purchased more recently and faced going into negative equity during their current tenure. They should be protected through tax subsidies and through regulation which prevents lenders from re-possessing homes, particularly of people still able to pay the mortgage. Where mortgage payments become a problem lenders should be required to re-schedule debts by extending repayment periods, as is the normal practice in France and other continental European countries. This might be hard to impose now, since people mortgage at such high multiples of earnings, unlike in a country like France where the affordability limit is normally repayments at 30 percent of taxed income. But with lower prices mortgagees would less leveraged, and lenders might be more flexible about extending terms. Perhaps the main negative effect on home owners would be in the loss of collateral for further borrowing. But private debt is already at unsustainably high levels in the UK—higher than in almost any other OECD country—and more private borrowing for consumption should not be encouraged.

The principles behind capital gains tax on private property are fair and transparent and the effects would be economically and socially beneficial over the longer term. It is true that advocates of higher property taxation tend to favour alternative schemes, but these are either more complex or likely to be less efficacious. Labour and Liberal Democrat proposals at the 2010 election for a 'mansion tax' on properties worth more than two million pounds were little more than political posturing. It would have raised relatively little revenue and by carefully calibrating the threshold so that only the wealthy would be hit only avoided the key issue. To stop the continuing escalation of house prices and reduce generational inequalities we need to lessen the incentives for property speculation not only amongst the very rich but also amongst those in the middle who have also received substantial unearned gains through rising house prices.

Land-value taxes are also more favoured by many of the more perceptive commentators on the housing market and they do have some advantages. You are not taxing people on the value they add to their homes by investing in home improvement but only on the unearned value accruing through rises in the value of land (although you can achieve the same through CGT by allowing offsets on taxable profits for home improvements). Furthermore, the tax is imposed on land which is left unused while prices rise, and so discourages speculation based on rising land value. But these taxes would be complex to administer—requiring constant re-evaluations of the value of all properties in land, net of the value of the buildings. And they fail to address the main fiscal inequity in exempting one class of assets from taxation on profits on sale. One potential problem with CGT on all private property sales—the danger that it would cause a deficit of properties for sale as older people withdrew from the market to avoid the taxes—would be avoided by imposing a land-value tax rather than CGT. On the other hand, the danger of a market contraction in house sales following the introduction of CGT could be diminished in another way. We could simply reform the Council Tax so that people in higher value properties paid a higher price for keeping them.

REFORMING COUNCIL TAX

The Council Tax in England is currently in a mess. It is a tax imposed on individuals (with certain groups exempted) but it is both a personal and a property tax, where, in the latter case, the amount paid is calculated according the notional value of the property in which they live. Properties are divided into eight bands with progressively higher rates, with the top band charged at three times the bottom band. The trouble is that the rateable values date from 1992, since no government has followed through on the many promises made to update these values in

England (although they have in been Wales and Scotland). The result is that differential charges between the band rates bear no relation to the actual differentials in the values of people's homes today.

The bottom band 'A' is for properties valued in 1992 at up to £40,000 and the top 'H' band is for properties valued at £320,000 or more. In 1992 someone in an average A band property worth, say, £20,000, was paying one third of the rate of someone in a band H property which might have been worth £400,000. Their rates were set at a third of the charge for homes in band 'H', even though their properties might have been worth one twentieth of the value of the band H property. Since 1992 house prices have risen by around four times, and by more at the top end. So the top band would now include properties worth £7 million, while the average value of band A properties might be something in the region of £70,000. The value of the expensive property would be 100 times the value of the less expensive property, but the tax rate would still be only three times more. So the Council Tax is highly regressive and fails to tax the very wealthy at anything like an equitable rate for the value of their property. Research from the Joseph Rowntree Foundation from 2006 estimated what each household income quintile was paying on Council Tax as a proportion of its income. It found that households in the bottom quintile were paying on average 4.9 percent while those in the top quintile were paying only 1.7 percent.[7]

Clearly the bands need to be revised and many are campaigning for this but successive governments have been reluctant to act, presumably fearing a backlash from those in valuable properties who would be paying more. This should not be allowed to deter a reform which benefits the majority. The simple answer would be to add some new bands to the scale, to reflect the fact that there are now many more very expensive houses, and to revalue properties according to current prices. The Centre for Economic and Business Research recommends adding three new bands to create a new revalued A to K scale. Band A would be for homes now worth under £85,000 and band K for home worth more than £4 million. Their proposal would raise the ratio of top band to bottom band charges from the current 3:1 to 4.5:1. Band K property owners would see their council taxes rise to around £4493, some £1500 more than they currently pay.

This is a modest proposal which would raise an additional revenue of around £4.7 billion, considerably more than the mansion tax proposal would have raised. A more equitable solution, which would come closer to taxing property wealth on a proportionate and therefore more pro-gressive basis, would need to increase the ratio substantially more than this. According to the Joseph Rowntree Foundation research reported earlier, the ratio of charges between the old bands should have been closer to ten to one to be proportionate to the average incomes of peo-ple living in properties in each band. With more bands the ratio would need to be higher.

A reformed Council Tax system would have a number of clear ben-efits. Taxation in Britain is highly centralised with only some five percent of total tax being raised locally.[8] This addition to local taxation would help cash-starved local councils to continue to deliver essential services and fits well with the current Government's 'localism' agenda. The tax is easy to collect—with an estimated 97 percent collection rate in 2014— and, once the revaluation process was completed, would incur no extra charges to administer, until the next re-evaluation at least. Assuming that councils levied the tax on occupied and un-occupied property alike, as they should, it would provide a stronger dis-incentive to property devel-opers leaving their properties empty since they would be paying higher charges for the privilege. It would also act to counter any tendency to hoard properties that might arise from the wider imposition of capital gains tax. There are currently around 2.9 million homes occupied by the over 65s, with more than two extra bedrooms, and the Government is encouraging them to downsize to free up more family homes.[9] An extra tax on the profits from selling their homes would work against this. But having to pay substantially higher council taxes might encourage them to do so anyway, especially if stamp duty for the elderly buyer were scrapped as well. And the main benefit of course would be that the tax would be much more equitable than it is at present.

Some object that raising top end Council Tax will unfairly penalise cash-poor older people who have seen the value of their properties rise through no fault of the own. But the objection is misplaced. According to the Joseph Rowntree Foundation the number of low income pension-ers living in properties in the F to H bands is very small—only about 100,000 in 2005.[10] Many of these will have substantial care bills and will no doubt need to down-size their properties in any case to pay for their care in the new asset-based welfare system which is emerging in this country. Younger people, on the other hand, would benefit greatly from the downward pressure such reforms would exercise on house prices.

Measures like these to reduce property prices could be a risky business and would need to be managed carefully. A fall in borrowing and consumption among home-owners would be likely to follow an announcement of any such changes to property taxation. In the longer term, this would be balanced by increasing spending from the younger generations who currently have little to left spend after paying high rents and mortgages. However, there might be a bumpy ride for the economy and the changes would no doubt have to be implemented gradually. However, the long-term benefits would be considerable. Reducing house prices and investment in property would help to 're-balance' the economy and would certainly create more economic stability. It would also create a more equal society with smaller gaps in wealth and incomes. But most important, it would help to reduce intergenerational inequality. There is probably no more effective single way for achieving this than reducing house prices.

RE-REGULATING THE RENTAL SECTOR

At the same time, Britain needs to address the very real problems in the private rental sector. It is currently amongst the most de-regulated in Europe and, in today's normally boosterish housing market, this means rents are very high and quality and security often low. Many countries regulate rents to avoid exploitation of tenants. Even New York maintains rent control. Britain abolished its rent controls in the 1980s and has seen rents rise astronomically since the 1990s in areas where house prices are high. Any notion that greater competition in a less regulated rental market would keep prices lower has proven groundless.

De-regulation has also meant less security for tenants who under current tenancy law can be asked to leave by landlords at short notice (three months) and with no reason given. The average tenancy is now less than two years and many complain of being forced to leave as landlords continually hike the rents to levels they can't afford. Estate agents often connive in the process, encouraging landlords to raise prices annually, and to evict tenants who can't pay. In some cities they now demand fees for showing properties for rent and even require nine months advance payment of rents to tenants considered risky. Landlords, egged on by agents, frequently try to increase their profits at the end of tenancies by demanding large damage deductions from returnable deposits, even where such 'damage' is no more than normal 'wear and tear.' Fortunately, where tenants can afford the time to lodge appeals, tribunals often tend to find the landlord demands excessive. We are now treated to obnoxious Radio four advertisements from landlord insurers promising landlords to make any problems with pesky tenants 'go away.' The chosen advertsing medium says a lot about the demographics of landlords. Nothing better captures the shamelessly exploitative culture that has grown up around private renting in our times.

With the proportion of people in private rental tenures increasing so rapidly, and with abuses on the rise, this situation has to change. It is time for a new housing act that properly regulates the rental market, and ensures that private renters get a better deal. Rent controls need to re-introduced, at least in the larger cities, where rents are so high, so that the concept of 'fair rents' can begin to be restored. To give legitimate tenants greater security, legal notice periods should be revised so that landlords are obliged to give nine months notice to end a tenancy where no breach of tenancy agreements has occurred. New longer-term tenancy contracts should also be available with landlords obliged to grant these to established tenants with good records who wish to re-contract for longer periods. Where landlords seek to give notice to such tenants who may wish to apply for longer term tenancies, tenants should have the right to appeal, with landlords obliged to give just reasons as to why they should not extend contracts for tenants in compliance with their tenancy agreements.

Tenants with young children at local schools, for instance, who are paying their rents on time, and observing their tenancy agreements, should not have to leave at short notice simply because their landlord wants the house back for a relative or thinks it might be a good time to sell or to move back in to avoid paying CGT on a future sale. The concept of greater need should apply and local rent tribunals should be established to adjudicate it.

Landlords should be licensed, as are most other professionals providing essential services, and their properties should be subject to regular inspection, by bodies certified to do this. Newham Council has been successfully implementing such a scheme, bearing down on landlords who are letting illegally. It is only Government obstruction which is stopping this scheme being adopted by other councils. The law needs to uphold tenant's rights just as assiduously as it currently protects landlord's rights. Landlords must understand that they have responsibilities just as tenants do. Currently the balance between the two is seriously out of kilter. It needs to be restored by legislation.

CHAPTER 8

Political Power and Generational Prospects for the Future

Intergenerational inequality could be reaching a critical point in the UK, as in many other countries in Europe. As I have argued in this book, today's young people look set to be the first generation since the children of the Edwardian era with poorer life chances than their parents across a range of life domains. In housing, pensions and welfare benefits, they will almost certainly do worse over their lifetimes than the previous generation. In employment they have generally faced a difficult start to their adult lives, as age-related inequalities in unemployment and pay have risen, and with earnings and job quality for young people now in decline. Over time, many will catch up with their parents' generation in earnings, if not working conditions, but the less qualified are highly likely to fare worse than their parents throughout their lifetimes. It is only in education that we can say that generational opportunities have improved, but even here the benefits will be overshadowed by the declining value of qualifications on the labour market.

Some of the changes in life chances we have observed can be explained in terms of increasing inequalities. Inequalities in general have been rising in most spheres of social and economic life, including in earnings, housing and wealth. These inequalities show up as increasing gaps within age groups but also across age groups. So the gap between the old and the young grows consistently, in all areas, except education. But generational differences are cross-cut by social class divisions, which can easily obscure them. And it is important to remember this because political identities and allegiances are influenced, amongst other things, by both social class and generational differences.

© The Author(s) 2017
A. Green, *The Crisis for Young People*,
DOI 10.1007/978-3-319-58547-5_8

The majority of adults in the UK are pessimistic about the prospects for young people and expect that they will do worse over their lifetimes than their parents' generation. An international survey conducted by MORI in 2013 asked respondents: 'To what extent, if at all, do you think that today's youth will have had a better or worse life than their parents generation or will it be the same.'[1] Amongst adults in Great Britain 54 percent responded 'worse' and only 20 percent 'better'. The majority were pessimistic and more so than in most other countries surveyed. But not all young people and not all adults generally see things is this way. The same survey showed 61 percent in Great Britain 'optimistic' about the prospects 'for themselves and their family' over the coming year, with only 13 percent pessimistic. People in Britain tend to be more optimistic about their own future than the prospects for their social group in general. Our CELS survey results suggested that this was particularly true for young people. Better off respondents, not surprisingly, tend to be more optimistic than those worse off.

Many better-off parents who are able to support their children through unpaid internships and help them to buy homes, will deplore the difficulties faced by young people in general but are less likely to see these in terms of generational inequalities. After all, they are doing their best to mitigate the problems within their own families, even though this does nothing to reduce the problems of the less fortunate young people, whose parents are in no position to help. So for many people, wherever they lie on the political spectrum, the problems faced by young people today are the familiar ones of social class inequalities, with growing age-related inequalities being an additional but only temporary difficulty for young people. Their transitions to adult life will have been prolonged, but the lucky ones and the most 'resilient' will catch up in time.

The perspective is familiar and somehow reassuring, but does not fully capture the gravity of what is happening to the relationship between generations. Where a generation, on average, is likely to do worse than its parents' generation across many key domains and over the whole life course, a very major historical shift is occurring, and one that is unprecedented at least for the last century. We expect each generation to do better than the last. If that is no longer the case, it puts in question our whole notion of historical progress and indeed the viability of the current social and political order. It not only breaches the tacit social contract between generations. It also castes into doubt the socio-economic system which is designed, among other things, to maintain this generational contract.

When rising social class inequalities become intertwined with widening intergenerational inequality, there is a very large potential pool of people for whom 'the system is not working.' If the current young generation enter middle age in the mid 2020s still struggling to find homes and decent jobs, and if the prospects for those who follow look no better; if inequality is still rising in both wealth and incomes; and if a post-Brexit Britain is still mired in slow growth with high levels of both private and public debt; a political sea change may occur. Ten years from now, when population ageing is beginning to peak, may be a critical turning point. Of course, we do not have a crystal ball and cannot know this for sure. We cannot be certain that the current generation will have suffered a lifetime intergenerational decline for another 40 years. All we can do is to make predictions based on current trends, factoring in different contingencies. But the trends do not look good, either economically or politically.

Britain has barely recovered from the financial crisis of 2007/2008 which brought the most prolonged recession in living memory. Ten years after the onset of this financial cataclysm, GDP per capita has only just regained pre-recession levels; GDP growth remain slow, although currently better than in many OECD countries; business investment is anaemic; productivity improves glacially, and trade deficits are at an historical high.[2] The drastic financial measures adopted here, as elsewhere, to save the economic system are everywhere running out of road. Quantitative easing and near-zero interest rates, designed to increase liquidity and boost business confidence and consumer demand, seem to have a diminishing impact. Business investment remains stubbornly low, even if consumer demand is sustained by credit card purchasing in the UK. Because investment, both public and private, is so weak Britain's labour productivity remains relatively low—with output per hour worked still lagging France and Germany by a quarter.[3] This holds back the improvements in wages and living standards which, in any case, now everywhere struggle to track productivity improvements.[4] Britain's economy remains both sectorally and regionally unbalanced. Little has yet been achieved to rectify the problems which caused the Great Recession in the first place.

Regulators have made banks hold higher capital ratios and the banking system is supposedly more stable, but savings are low and declining, household debt is almost back to pre-recession levels, while the public debt continues to rise. As before the recession, demand remains dependent on high levels of household borrowing, not least through the mortgage debt which continues to increase with ever rising house prices. Further artificial boosts to the economy have come through the liberalisation of pensions in 2015, allowing over-55 private pension holders to cash in on their pension pots at will. But the benefits will be short-term and come at a price, storing up problems for the future funding of old age.

The same short-termism applies to many of the financial measures used to stave off financial collapse. Quantitative easing enhanced liquidity and demand, temporally, but creates asset bubbles which ramp up the inequality which is a major cause of suppressed demand and persisting low growth in the economy. The less affluent, who spend most of what they earn, have little more to spend, while the richest ten percent, who have captured most of the earnings growth in recent decades, can find little left to buy, and hoard their money, mostly in 'unproductive' property assets.[5] Meanwhile, efforts to curb excessive pay in the banking sector have failed dismally, with bankers' bonuses now back to the their pre-crisis peak. Whereas many institutions and individuals deemed to have contributed to the US banking collapse in 2008 have been subject to legal proceedings and large financial penalties, few corporate heads have rolled in Britain, and there remains a pervasive culture of dishonest practices in the banking system.[6]

The dysfunctional model of financialised, neo-liberal capitalism, which nearly brought down the global economy, carries on, zombie-like. Short of some final-hour rethink by European leaders on the EU's free labour movement policy—clearly disliked by substantial majorities in the northwest European countries—proponents of Brexit can propose no credible economic alternative. Stripped of the bombast about a new global Britain, we are, in effect, offered the prospect an insular Little Britain, marooned politically and economically somewhere in the mid-Atlantic, and just desperately trying to stay afloat, competing as an offshore tax haven with a race to the bottom on regulation and corporate taxation.

These economic problems are not, of course, unique to Britain. Advanced economies the world over are struggling with ageing populations, high unemployment and slow growth. What Wolfgang Streeck calls the 'three horsemen of contemporary capitalism'—stagnation, debt and inequality—are continuing to stalk the economic and political landscape.[7] The financialised turbo-capitalism of the 'roaring nineties' and early 2000s begins to look like the last throw of the dice for the model of liberal market capitalism which has dominated the global era.

For a while it looked like this new model had found a way to transcend the endemic contradictions of the post-industrial world. After the years of declining rates of growth, shrinking investment opportunities, and the 'profits squeeze' which characterised the late Keynesian era and came to a head with the stagflation and oil price hikes of the 1970s,[8] capitalism managed to reinvent itself in the 1980s. De-regulation of domestic and international markets, including most importantly in finance, combined with the opportunities offered by the new communications and information technologies, brought a surge in world trade and the rise of the mighty new transnational corporations that came to dominate the world economy. Unable to globalise like capital, constrained by domestic political assaults, and with workers vulnerable to the off-shoring of jobs, trades unions were substantially weakened. The labour share of income declined whilst the capital share rose.[9] Capital found new markets for investment and profit, not least in the service industries which compliant governments were only too happy to privatise. Markets were aggressively expanded, commodifying all areas of life, including those previously deemed more suited to public management. Then, when the end-of-Millennium dot.com bubble burst signalled the failure of the new technologies to deliver the expected productivity gains, financialisation was ramped up to a higher gear, with super-profits now derived through speculative transactions and new financial instruments operating outside of the 'real economy'. With financial speculation focused above all on property, there was a new era of debt-fuelled growth which came to its inevitable demise, as we know, with the 2008 financial crisis.

It is hard now to see where this discredited experiment in finacialised market capitalism can go next. It has failed to solve the problems of economic stagnation and declining rates of productivity growth. The government austerity programmes, enacted almost everywhere in the wake of the crisis, have failed to tackle the problems of rising public debt. Ageing populations, excessive private debt, and ever-rising income inequality all continue to bear down on the demand needed for re-booting growth. There are few areas of social life remaining for profitable marketisation; little room is left for the further exploitation of labour; and the limits of financial speculation have surely been reached. With the increasing corporate take-over of the democratic process,[10] the marginalisation of counter ideologies to market liberalism, and the weakening of oppositional forces in a global world that structurally favours international capital, it is hard to see from where change will come. Even the gradual eastward shift of the global centre of economic gravity[11] seems unlikely to throw up a new model of capitalism capable of global economic leadership. As Streeck comments: 'no force is at hand that could be expected to reverse the three down trends in economic growth, social equality and financial stability and end their mutual reinforcement.'[12] Whereas historically capitalism has been helped to survive by the constraints imposed on it by non-market forces, institutions and ideologies, these are no longer so effective. Capitalist progress has by now, says Streeck, more or less destroyed any agency capable of stabilising it.

Globalisation was never the one-way historical street described by the globalists.[13] It has already—let us not forget—gone decisively into retreat at least once, with the eclipse of liberalism during the period of the two world wars.[14] Now, engulfed by new contradictions, it appears in danger of switching to reverse gear again. 20 years ago two very prescient journalists gave the following millennial warning. '(T)he foremost task of democratic politicians on the threshold of the next century,' they wrote,

> will be to restore the state and the primacy of politics over economics. If this is not done, the dramatic fusing together of humanity through technology and trade will soon turn into the opposite and lead to global crack-up.[15]

The warnings were not headed—in fact the state and political elites became ever more supine in the face of global corporate power—and we are at this prophetic point now. That globalisation is in crisis was never more evident than in the calamitous events of 2016. Regional war, terrorism, the humanitarian disaster of millions refugees bringing the crisis back home to the West, where in part it originated, all cast a dark shadow over this tragic year. The UK referendum vote for Brexit, and the election of a right-wing, nationalist demagogue to the world's most powerful office, sounded a wake-up call to the liberal order; and there will be more political shocks to come. Both proclaim the reassertion of politics and the (nation) state against the might of the global markets, supposedly in the name of the 'sovereign people.' But this is not happening in the way that most western critics of global market capitalism would have wanted. The new proponents of nationalism and protectionism are still backed, behind the scenes, by corporate power, particularly in the US, where President Trump has already stuffed his administration with the same Wall Street big moneymen he derided during the election complain. The resurgent Leviathan slouches in from the Right, not the Left.

It may be that some new technological breakthrough will break the economic impasse we seem to have reached. There may be a new general purpose technology like, in their time, steam power, electrification, and the transistor which enabled the micro-processor revolution, modern computing and the internet. Some think that artificial intelligence and robotisation will be of this order.[16] They would certainly offer technological improvements in a wide range of new products and processes—rather more so than the often paltry inventions of the digital economy in our era, like facebook, and the rest of the social media. But for many economists they also seem likely to be a massive job killers, particularly when robots start designing and building new robots. We are hardly ready for such a massive labour displacement when the world population continues its rapid rise.

The overall outlook in the UK, as in the developed world generally, is bleak for most people—of all ages. But we can expect that the political elites in the UK, at least, will continue, as they have done since the crisis, to ensure that the young carry the heaviest burden.

GERONTOCRACY AND POLITICS

We are living in an ageing society which increasingly resembles gerontocracy—a society where power lies with the old. Age-related inequalities in political power are growing and for the foreseeable future advantage the baby-boomer generation over successor generations. This is partly because some birth cohorts are bigger than others and the baby boomers were a particularly large generation, thus having inflated power within the political process. But it is mostly because the electorate generally is ageing due to longer life expectancy. The median age of the electorate has been rising since the 1990s, with 44 being the median age in the 1991 election and 46 in the 2010 election. Craig Berry's demographic projections for the Intergenerational Foundation suggest that the electorate will continue to age at least until 2051, so that the median age rises to 47 in 2021; 50 in 2041; and 51 in 2051.[17]

It is also well-known that older age groups are more likely to register and to turn-out in elections. According to MORI the actual turn-out by age group in 2010 was 44 percent for 18–24s; 55 percent for 25–34s, compared with 73 percent for 55–64s and 76 percent for the over 65s.[18] The over 65s were almost twice as likely to vote as 18–24 year olds. This means that the actual voting power of older groups relative to younger ones tends to be even higher than their relative electoral strength. The median actual voter in 2010 was 49, whereas the median member of the electorate was 46. According to Berry's projections, based on the recent turn-out rates of different age groups, the median actual voter will be 52 in 2021 and 54 in 2051. People with different types of housing tenure also show a differential propensity to vote. In 2010, 89 percent of outright owners voted; 87 percent of mortgagees; 78 percent of social housing tenants; and only 56 percent of private renters.[19] Given that young people are increasingly likely to be renting privately, and make up the majority of private renters, this also bodes badly for the 'voting power' of younger people.

The ageing of the electorate matters because voter political preferences vary by age and because there is a degree of 'generational selfishness' in voting patterns. Furlong and Cartmel's analysis of the 2009/2010 British Election Survey showed clear age-related patterns on a number of issues. Amongst Millennial respondents, for instance, 57 percent of females and 49 percent of males listed unemployment amongst the three most important issues. Amongst baby boomers only 40 percent of women and 33 percent of men did so.[20] Other more recent analyses of age biases in policy preferences, also show older people being more likely to support the NHS than younger people, and younger people more likely to prioritise education.[21] Older voters were, of course, much more likely to support Brexit than younger voters. With the increasing power of the grey vote, and a mainstream media which reflects their preferences, it is highly likely that governments will favour policies which appeal to these demographics.

In recent years government pandering to the grey vote has become, arguably, ever more explicit. Recent governments have prioritised spending on health, while cutting back on services for young children (Sure Start) and adolescents (further education, the Careers Service, youth clubs etc.); they have maintained a 'triple lock' on pensions whilst driving down the value of other benefits (working family tax credits; education maintenance allowances; housing benefits) which are used more by the young; they have continued to subsidize TV licenses and winter fuel costs for those over 65s, even though this age group is now on average better off than those in their 20s; and they have kept interest rates and inflation low, which benefits older people by supporting the growth in the value of the homes, and by helping to maintain the real value of the savings, even where the interest accumulated is low. At the same time, governments have failed to regulate the private housing market on which young people are more dependent. Even the much detested 'spare room tax' contains exemptions for older people. Rising tuition fees and living costs for students, paid from student loans, saddles new generations with high levels of debt, but other policies were available for making graduates contribute more for the education higher education from which they benefit. The proposals for a proper graduate tax to be levied on all graduate tax payers who had studied free of charge in English universities, would have been much less discriminatory by age, as well as by social class, but was never seriously considered.

Given the increasing age-bias of government policies it is hardly surprising that young people are less and less inclined to vote. It is not so much that they are 'apathetic' or 'disinterested' in politics, as in the usual media stereotype. It is more a question of mainstream political parties having nothing to say to their interests. Young people feel they are not represented. Henn and Ford's survey of 18 year olds in 2011 found 63 percent of respondents claiming to be 'interested in politics.' Yet over half agreed that 'young people like me have no say in what Government does' (with 14 percent disagreeing) and 61 percent agreed that they had 'little or no influence on decisions made on their behalf by governments'. Over half of the respondents believed that governments treat young people unfairly (15 percent disagreed).[22] The findings of our 2014 CELS survey broadly concurred with this picture of young people remaining engaged in political issues but demoralised by their lack of voice in electoral politics (Keating et al. 2015).

The ageing of the British electorate is likely to continue to deepen age-related inequalities in (electoral) political power as time goes on. So long as mainstream political parties look no further than winning the next election, and respond only to the messages from focus groups and pollsters on how to fashion their policies to maximise electoral gains, governments are likely to continue to implement measures which reduce young people's opportunities and deepen the age-related inequalities we have discussed throughout this book.

The Millennials will have been a particularly unlucky generation, not just because of the material circumstances of period in which they were born and grew up, but also because their political power has been eclipsed by an ageing electorate. The generation which follows them may do no better. But the coming of the gerontocratic society portends stark changes not just for today's and tomorrow's young people, but for society as a whole. Younger people tend to want to invest in the future—they and their children are the future. Their elders want to enjoy what they have left and focus on the shorter horizon. Arguably, it is only the intergenerational bond which mitigates the presentism of the elderly.[23] If this is starting to weaken, then an individualistic and conservative gerontocratic state would take less and less care to invest in the future.

This electoral arithmetic certainly looks bleak. However, there is another scenario to counter this pessimistic vision. It focuses not so much on the divide between the young and the old, but on what is happening in between and on what one may call 'youth crisis age creep'. Older voters may continue to dominate electoral politics but still almost half of the electorate will remain under 50. As time goes on, that younger half of the electorate, including those in early middle age, may well come to share more common interests, as the disadvantages currently experienced by 20 somethings become also the problems of those in their 40s.

In ten years time, the current generation in their 20s and early 30s begin to reach early middle age. If they are still mostly unable to buy houses and struggling to meet their rental and student loans payments; if many have still not achieved jobs commensurate with their educational qualifications and are 'just managing' in precarious jobs with declining conditions and pay; and if those coming behind are doing no better; then a powerful new electoral alliance could emerge across age groups, capable of challenging the power of the gerontocratic electorate.

Radical policies on housing—such as capital gains tax on first homes sales; council tax reforms; re-regulation of the rental sector—which currently appeal mostly to younger age groups, might then be in the interests of wide swathes of the electorate under 45. A small increment in income tax for graduates, in return for the writing off of their student debt, may seem like a good deal to the 40 something graduates with families who are still paying off student loans at the same time as paying high rents and mortgages. Equally, as precarious working becomes the norm across age groups, there might be substantial majorities in favour of labour market reform to return stability and dignity to working life.

These voices would have to be heard. The media could not stereotype this younger half of the adult population as lazy or disengaged youngsters. They would now be the majority of the economically active, whose labour and taxes were paying the pensions and care of those in older age.

They would still be the future—but also the main guarantors of what's left of the current social system. A lot will depend on how their political aspirations evolve over the turbulent years into which we now enter.

NOTES

CHAPTER ONE

1. See respectively the titles of the following: Allen, M. and Ainley, P. *Lost Generation? New Strategies for Youth and Education.* Continuum, London, 2010; Howker, E. and Malik, S. *Jilted Generation. How Britain has Bankrupted its Youth.* Icon Books, London, 2013; Gould, G. *Wasted: How Misunderstanding Young People Threatens Our Future.* Abacus, London, 2015; Gardiner, L. *Stagnation Generation: The Case for Renewing the Intergenerational Contract.* Resolution Foundation, July 2016, p.25. See also: Putnam, R. *Our Kids: The American Dream in Crisis.* Simon and Schuster, New York, 2015; Willetts, D. *The Pinch: How the Baby Boomers Took their Children's Future—and Why They Should Give It Back.* Atlantic Books, London, 2010.
2. See: Green, A. and Janmaat, J-G. *Regimes of Social Cohesion: Societies and the Crisis of Globalisation.* Palgrave, Basingstoke, 2011; Judt, T. *Ill Fares the Land,* Penguin Books, 2010 and Gardeiner, op. cit.
3. See: Schoon, I. and Bynner, J. (eds) *Young People and the Great Recession: Preparing for an Uncertain Future,* Cambridge University Press, Cambridge, 2017; Smets, K. 'Revisiting the Political Life-Cycle: Later Maturation and Turn-out Decline Amongst Young Adults,' *European Political Science Review,* 2015, pp. 1-25.
4. See: Silver, J. *Coming Up Short: Working-Class Adulthood in an Age of Uncertainty.* Oxford University Press, Oxford, 2013.
5. Ibid.
6. ONS data: http://www.ons.gov.uk/ons/rel/lifetables/decennial-life-tables/english-life-tables–no-17–2010-12/stb-elt17.html

© The Editor(s) (if applicable) and The Author(s) 2017   133
A. Green, *The Crisis for Young People,*
DOI 10.1007/978-3-319-58547-5

7. Office for National Statistics. *Statistical Bulletin. Mortality Assumptions: 2010-based National Population Projections.* Appendix A, England tables, October 2011.

8. Howker and Malik, op. cit. p. 51.

9. See Willetts, op. cit.

10. See: ONS, Population and Migration. Dependency ratios. Figure 2 at: http://www.ons.gov.uk/ons/guide-method/compendiums/compendium-of-uk-statistics/population-and-migration/find-out-more/index.html.

11. See: Hills, J. *Good Times, Bad Times. The Welfare Myth of Them and US.* Bristol Policy Press, 2015.

12. See: Willetts, op. cit.

13. Ibid.

14. Ibid.

15. See: Esping-Andersen, G. 'Inequality of Incomes and Opportunities' in A. Giddens and P. Diamond (eds) *The New Egalitarianism.* Polity Press, Cambridge, 2005; Thurow, L. *The Future of Capitalism.* Nicholas Brearley Publishing, London, 1996.

16. See: Crouch, C. *The Knowledge Corrupters: Hidden Consequences of the Financial Takeover of Public Life.* Polity Press, Cambridge, 2016; Hutton, W. *Them and Us: Changing Britain—Why We Need a Fairer Society.* Little Brown, London, 2010.

17. See: Glyn, A. *Capitalism Unleashed: Finance, Globalisation and Welfare.* Oxford University Press, Oxford, 2017.

18. See: Felstead, A., Gallie, D. and Green, F. *Unequal Britain at Work.* Oxford University Press, Oxford, 2015.

19. Standing, G. *The Precariat: The Dangerous New Class.* Bloomsbury Academic, London, 2011.

20. See: Blossfeld, H.-P., Klitjzing, E., Mills, M. and Kurtz, K. *Globalization, Uncertainty and Youth in Society.* Routledge, London, 2005.

21. Bell, D. and Blanchflower, D. *Young People and the Great Recession.* Discussion Paper No. 5674. Bonn. IZA, 2011.

22. Brown, P., Lauder, H. and Ashton, D. *The Global Auction: The Broken Promises of Education, Jobs, and Incomes.* Oxford University Press, New York, 2011.

23. See: Harvey, D. 'The Right to the City,' *New Left Review,* 53, 2008; Green, A., Mostafa, T. and Preston, J. *The Chimera of Competitiveness: Varieties of Capitalism and the Economic Crisis.* LLAKES Research Paper 8. LLAKES Centre, UCL Institute of Education, London, 2010; Stiglitz, J. *Freefall: Free Markets and the Sinking of the Global Economy.* Penguin, Allen Lane, London, 2010.

24. See: Schoon and Bynner. op. cit.; Schoon and Lyons-Amos, 2015.

25. See: Smetz, op.cit.

26. Thurow, op. cit.
27. See: Crouch, C. *The Strange Non- Death of Neo-liberalism*, Polity, 2011; Stiglitz, J. 2012. *The Price of Inequality*. W. W. Norton and Company, New York; Stiglitz, 2010.
28. See: Brown et al., 2011, op. cit.
29. See: Dorling, D. *Inequality and the 1 percent*, Verso, London, 2014; Dorling, D. *Injustice: Why Social Inequality Still Persists*. Policy Press, Bristol, 2010; Hutton, 2010, op. cit. and Hutton, W. *How Good We Can Be*. Abacus, 2014, p. 113.
30. See: Esping-Andersen, G. *The Incomplete Revolution*, Polity Press, Cambridge, 2009; Esping-Andersen, 2005, op. cit; Willetts, 2010, op. cit.
31. Piketty, 2014, op. cit.
32. Ibid.
33. See: Dorling, 2010, op. cit.
34. See: Willetts, 2010, op. cit.
35. Putnam, 2015, op. cit.
36. See: Willetts, op. cit.
37. See: Piketty, T. *Capital in the Twenty-First Century*. Belknap, Harrvard, 2014.
38. Hobsbawm, E. *Age of Extremes. The Short Twentieth Century, 1914–1991*. Abacus, London, 1995.
39. See: Green, F. and Zhu, Y. 'Overqualification, Job Dissatisfaction, and Increasing Dispersion inthe Returns to Graduate Education,' *Oxford Economic Papers* 62, 4, 2010 pp. 740–763.
40. See: Standing, op. cit.
41. Howker and Malik, op. cit.
42. Gould, op. cit.
43. See also: Hutton, 2011, op. cit.
44. National Audit Office. 2016. *Taxpayer Support for UK Banks*. Accessed, 25.8.2016, at: https://www.naohttps://www.ipsos-mori.com/researchpub-lications/researcharchive/3754/Social-mobility-stalls-as-housing-dreams-are-dashed.aspx.org.uk/highlights/taxpayer-support-for-uk-banks-faqs/;.
45. Willetts, op. cit.

CHAPTER TWO

1. See: Institute of Manpower Studies. *Competence and Competition*. Manpower Services Commission, London, 1984; Green, A. *Education and State Formation. The Rise of Education Systems in England, Europe and the USA*. Macmillan, London, 1990.

2. See: European Commission. *A Memorandum on Lifelong Learning,*
   2000. Accessed 10 June 2016 at: http://europa.eu.int/comm/educa-
   tion/life/memoen.pfd; European Commission. *White Paper: Teaching*
   and Learning—Towards the Learning Society. European Commission,
   Brussels, 1995; Green, A. 'Lifelong Learning and the Learning Society:
   Different European Models of Organization' in A. Hodgson (ed)
   Policies, Politics and the Future of Lifelong Learning, Kogan Page, 2000,
   pp. 35–50; Green, A. 'The Many Faces of Lifelong Learning: Recent
   Education Policy Trends in Europe', *Journal of Education Policy* 17, 6,
   2003, pp. 611–626; OECD *Lifelong Learning for All.* OECD, Paris,
   1996.

3. See: Crouch, C., Finegold, D. and Sako, M. *Are Skills the Answer?: The*
   Political Economy of Skill Creation in Advanced Industrial Countries.
   Oxford University Press, New York, 1999. Department of Trade and
   Industry. White Paper: *Our Competitive Future: Building the Knowledge*
   Driven Economy. DTI, London, 1998; Reich, R. *The Work of Nations: A*
   Blueprint for the Future. Simon and Schuster, London, 1991.

4. See: Brown, P., Green, A. and Lauder, H. *High Skills: Globalization,*
   Competitiveness and Skills Formation. Oxford University Press, Oxford,
   2001.

5. See: Allen and Ainley, op. cit.cit.

6. See: Brown et al., 2011, op. cit.

7. See: Bolton, P. *Education: Historical Statistics Standard Note:* SN/
   SG/4252 Last updated: 27 November 2012. Social & General Statistics,
   House of Commons library. file:///C:/Users/tedpaag/Downloads/
   SN04252.pdf

8. Department for Education (DFE), *Statistical First Release: Participation*
   in Education, Training and Employment by 16–18 Year Olds in England:
   End 2014. DFE, London, 2015.

9. Data sources: for 2000s, data are from OECD, *Education at a Glance,*
   OECD, Paris 2013b, p. 37, Table A1.3a; for 1980s, data are from
   OECD, *Education at a Glance.* OECD, Paris, 2010, p. 36, Table A1.3a.
   The OECD give us the tertiary graduation rate for the UK in 2010 as
   60 percent but this is calculated using a different methodology from
   the pre-2005 series.

10. Comparable OECD data are not yet available for this year becase based
    on reported qualifications at 30–34 years.

11. Mizen, P. *Young People's Experience of the Youth Training Scheme: A*
    Case Study of Recent State Intervention in the Youth Labour Market.
    Submitted for the degree of Ph.D., University of Warwick, Department
    of Sociology, September, 1990, p. 23.

12. See: Raffe, D., Brannen, K., Fairgrieve, J. and Martin, C.. 'Participation, Inclusiveness, Academic Drift and Parity of Esteem: a Comparison of Post-Compulsory Education and Training in England, Wales, Scotland and Northern Ireland.' *Oxford Review of Education*, 27, 2, 2001, pp. 173–203.

13. Research from the Institute of Fiscal Studies (IFS) suggested that in 56 of the 150 Local Education Authorities where they were piloted the EMA increased participation amongst eligible groups by 5.9 percent. See BBC: http://news.bbc.co.uk/1/hi/education/3638739.stm.

14. See: Thurow, op. cit.

15. See: Standing, op. cit.

16. See: Green, A. *Education and State Formation: Europe, East Asia and the USA*. Revised and Extended Second Edition. Palgrave, Basingstoke, 2013.

17. See: OECD. *Classifying Educational Programmes: Manual for ISCED-97 Implementation in OECD Countries*. OECD, Paris, 1999.

18. OECD reporting assigns qualifications to ISCED levels according to the attributions made by country authorities. We exclude from Level 3 in England those whose highest qualification has been classified as ISCED 3C (≥ 2), since this category includes many qualifications, like GCSEs, GNVQ Intermediate, BTEC First, NVQ 2 and City and Guilds Level 2, which can either be taken during lower secondary education, or require less than 2 years of upper secondary education. For other countries in the survey, qualifications classified to ISEC 3 C (≥ 2) include only those for which the earliest age of completion is 17 or 18 years, whereas for England the minimum age at which the above qualification can be gained is noted (correctly) as 16 years.

19. See: Sullivan, A., Heath, A. and Rothon, C. 'Equalisation or Inflation? Social Class and Gender Differentials in England and Wales.' *Oxford Review of Education*, 37, 2, 2001, pp. 215–240; Wolf, A. *Fixing a Broken Training System: The Case for an Apprenticeship Levy*. Social Market Foundation, London, 2015.

20. See: Jerrim, J. and Shure, N. *Achievement of 15-Year Olds in England: PISA 2015 National Report*, DFE, December 2016; OECD PISA reports from 2000 to 2016.

21. See: Green, A., Green, F. and Pensiero, N. *Why are Literacy and Numeracy Skills in England so Unequal? Evidence from the OECD's Survey of Adult Skills and Other International Surveys*. LLAKES Research Paper 47. UCL Institute of Education, London, 2014.

22. Department of Business, Innovation and Skills (BIS) *The International Survey of Adult Skills: Adult Literacy, Numeracy and Problem-Solving*

Skills in England. BIS Research Paper No. 139, BIS, London, 2013, p. 154.

23. Ibid.
24. See: Thomas, V., Wang, Y. and Fan, X. *Measuring Education Inequality: Gini Coefficients of Education*, World Bank Working Paper, World Bank, Washington, 2000.
25. Meschi, E., Scervini, F. *Expansion of Schooling and Educational Inequality in Europe: Educational Kuznets Curve Revisited.* GINI Discussion Paper N. 61, Amsterdam Institute for Advanced Labour Studies, Amsterdam, 2012.
26. Shavit, Y. and Blossfeld, H-P. *Persistent Inequality: Changing Educational Attainment in Thirteen Countries.* Chicago University Press, Chicago, 1993.
27. See: Ballarino, G. Bratti, M., Filippin, A., Fiorio, C., Leonardi, M. and Scervini, F. 'Increasing Educational Inequalities?' in Salverda, W., Nolan, B., Checchi, D., Marx, I. McKnight, A. Tóth, I. and van de Werfhorst, H. (eds) *Changing Inequalities in Rich Countries: Analytical and Comparative Perspectives*, Oxford University Press, Oxford, 2014; Breen, R., Luijkx, R. Müller, W. and Pollak, R. 'Non-Persistent Inequality in Educational Attainment: Evidence from Eight European Countries.' *American Journal of Sociology 114* (5), 2009, pp. 1475–521.
28. Sullivan, A. et al., op cit.
29. Green, A, Green, F. and Pensiero, N. 'Cross-Country Variation in Adult Skills Inequality: Why are Skill Levels and Opportunities so Unequal in Anglophone Countries?' *Comparative Education Review*, 59, 4, 2015, pp. 595–618.
30. See: Green, Green, and Pensiero, 2014, op cit.
31. Ibid.
32. See: OECD. *Skills Outlook 2013: First Results from the Survey of Adult Skill.* OECD, Paris, 2013a, p. 61.
33. Boudon, R. *Education, Opportunity and Social Inequality.* John Wiley and Sons, London, 1974.
34. Jackson, M. (ed) *Determined to Succeed? Performance versus Choice in Educational Attainment.* Stanford University Press, Stanford, 2013.
35. Raftery, A. E. and Hout, M. 'Maximally Maintained Inequality— Expansion, Reform, and Opportunity in Irish Education, 1921–75, *Sociology of Education*, 66, 1993, pp. 41–62.
36. Lucas, S. 'Effectively Maintained Inequality: Education Transitions, Track Mobility, and Social Background Effects,' *American Journal of Sociology*, 106, 6, 2001, pp. 1642–1690.
37. See: Allen and Ainley, op. cit.; Marginson, S. 'Global Stratification in Higher Education' in S. Slaughter and B. Taylor (eds). *Higher Education, Stratification and Workforce Development: Competitive advantage in Europe, the US and Canada.* Springer, Dordrecht, 2015.

38. Green, A. and Pensiero, N. 'The Effects of Upper-Secondary Education and Training Systems on Skills Inequality. A Quasi-Cohort Analysis Using PISA 2000 and the OECD Survey of Adult Skills.' *British Education Research Journal, 2016*, pp. 756–779.

39. At Level 3 alone, students in England in the 16 to 18 age group can choose among 3,729 qualifications. See: Hupkau, C., McNally, S., Ruiz-Valenzuela, J. and Ventura, G. *Post-Compulsory Education in England: Choices and Implications*, Discussion Paper 001. Centre for Vocational Education Research, LSE, London, 2016.

40. For those taking Applied Generals and Tech level courses at 17 in 2009, the percentage going on to commence a bachelor's degree was 29 and 26 percent respectively. A further 8 and 12 percent pursued non-bachelor Level 4 and above courses of study by the age of 20. See: Ibid.

41. Based on an analysis of linked data administrative data Hupkau et al. (ibid) show that amongst those following a Level 2 qualification at age 17 in 2009, 29 percent were observed working at this level for 2 years, 11 percent for 3 years and 3 percent for 4 years.

42. For those pursuing Level 2 qualifications at age 17 there is no clear trajectory to higher subsequent levels of learning. Most people classified as pursuing Level 2 qualifications at age 17 do not progress any higher up the education qualification ladder: only about 44 percent achieve a Level 3 qualification by the age of 20 (Ibid, p. 5).

43. See: Chartered Institute of Professional Development (CIPD). *Over-qualification and Skills Mismatch in the Graduate Labour Market*. Policy Report. CIPD, London, 2015.

44. See: OECD 2013b. *op. cit.*, Tables A6.2a and A6.2b.

45. See: Greenwood, C., Jenkins, A. and Vignoles, A. *The Returns to Qualifications in England: Updating the Evidence Base on Level 2 and Level 3 Vocational Qualifications*. London School of Economics, London, 2007.

46. Department for Business, Innovation and Skills (BIS) *Returns to Intermediate and Low Level Vocational Qualifications—Adding to the Existing Evidence Base*. BIS Research Paper 53. BIS, London, 2011.

47. Ibid.

48. Green and Pensiero, 2016, op. cit.

CHAPTER THREE

1. See: Bell and Blanchflower, op. cit.; Gregg, P., Machin, S. and Fernández-Salgado, M. 'The Squeeze On Real Wages—And What It Might Take To End It.' *National Institute of Economic Review*, 228, 1, 2014, pp. R3–R16; Willetts, op. cit.

2. Bell and Blanchflower, op. cit. pp. 25–26.
3. Gregg et al., 2014, p. 7.
4. Bell and Blanchflower, op. cit., pp. 25–27.
5 Bell and Blanchflower, op. cit., p. 26.
6. Kingman, D. and Seager, A. *Squeezed Youth: The Intergenerational Pay Gap and the Cost of Living Crisis.* Intergenerational Foundation, London, 2014, p. 6.
7. Willetts, op. cit., p. 69.
8. Hutton, 2014, op. cit. p. 113.
9. Standing, op. cit.
10. Felstead et al., op. cit.
11. Warren and Lyonette, op. cit.
12. Howker and Malik, op. cit., p. 136.
13. See: Streeck, W. *How Will Capitalism End?* Verso, London, 2016.
14. Confederation of British Industry/Pearson. *Changing the Pace: CBI Employment and Skills Survey,* 2013, p. 56.
15. See: Milburn, A. *Fair Access to Professional Careers. A Progress Report by the Independent Reviewer on Social Mobility and Child Poverty.* Accessed 11.10.2016 at: https://www.gov.uk/government/uploads/system/uploads/attachment_data/file/61090/IR_FairAccess_acc2.pdf.
16. Sutton Trust, *Internship or Indenture.* Sutton Trust Research Brief, 2014.
17. See: Gould, op cit, cited p. 194.
18. This section draws on interviews conducted in 2014/15 with some 100 young people in England aged 22–26. The core sample was drawn from the Citizenship Education Longitudinal Survey, with additions of young people recruited through snowballing and contacts with various youth agencies. The sample was reasonably representative by gender, region, and social background, although there was a slight over-representation of graduates. Names of respondents have been anonymised.
19. Brown et al., 2010, op. cit.
20. Gardiner, op. cit., p. 25.
21. See: Streeck, op. cit.

CHAPTER FOUR

1. 53 percent of those now aged 60 owned houses by the time they were 30. See: Lowe, S. *The Housing Debate.* Policy Press, Bristol, 2011, p. 178.
2. See: Dorling, D. *All that is Solid.* Allen Lane, London, 2014.
3. See ONS figures: http://webarchive.nationalarchives.gov.uk/20160105160709/. http://www.ons.gov.uk/ons/rel/census/2011-census-analysis/do-the-demographic-and-socio-economic-characteristics-of-those-living-alone-in-england-and-wales-differ-from-the-general-population-/sty-living-alone-in-the-uk.html.

4. Willetts, op. cit., p. 26.
5. Howker and Malik, op. cit.
6. Dorling, 2014, op. cit., p. 98.
7. Department for Communities and Local Goverment. Press Release: 'The Number of Newly Built Homes has Increased 6 percent in the Past Year.' August 25th, 2016. Accessed on 26.11.2016 at: https://www.gov.uk/government/news/increase-in-number-of-new-homes-built-and-started.
8. H.M. Government. White Paper: *Fixing Our Broken Housing Market*, February, 2017, p. 36. para 2.1.
9. Rebecca Tunstall cited by Dorling, 2014, op. cit. p. 201.
10. Dorling, 2014, op. cit., p. 196.
11. See: Armstrong, G. 'Commentary: UK Housing Market: Problems and Policies.' *National Institute Economic Review*, 235, February, 2016.
12. Dorling, 2014, op. cit., p. 47.
13. Rebecca Tunstall cited by Dorling, 2014, op. cit., p. 198.
14. Dorling, 2014, op. cit., p. 2001.
15. Collinson, P. 'But-to-Let Return of 16.3 percent Dwarfs other Investments', *The Guardian*, 26, 4, 2014, p. 37. See also Armstrong, op. cit.
16. See: Armstrong, op. cit.
17. Quoted by Howker and Malik, op. cit., p. 72.
18. See: Armstrong, op. cit.; and Lowe, op. cit.
19. See: Armstrong, op. cit.
20. See: See H.M. Government 2017, p. 10; Dorling, 2014, op. cit; Osborne, H. 'London Property now Costs 14 Times Average Wage,' *The Guardian*, November 25th, 2016, p. 37.
21. Howker and Malik, op. cit., p. 72.
22. H.M. Government, 2017, op. cit., p. 58, para 4.1.
23. See Willetts, 2010, op. cit.
24. Ibid, p.220.
25. Howker and Malik, op. cit., p. 66.
26. See: Willetts, 2010, p. 218.
27. See: Clapham, D., Mackie, P., Orford, S., Buckley, K. and Thomas, I. *Housing Options and Solutions for Young People in 2020*. Joseph Rowntree Foundation, 2012. file:///C:/Users/tedpaag/Downloads/young-people-housing-options-full_0.pdf. The National Housing Federation (NHF) indicated that the average single 21-year-old who regularly saves, receives no additional financial support and has no children will be 43 before being able to buy a first home based on a 20 percent deposit (NHF, 2010). Currently, low-to-middle earners can expect to spend up to 31 years saving in order to make their first purchase, based on saving 5 percent of their net income (Alakeson, 2011).
28. Howker and Malik, op. cit., pp. 2–13.

29. Lowe, op. cit., p. 125.
30. Clapham et al., 2012, op. cit., p. 17.
31. See: Crook, A. and Kemp, P. *Private Landlords in Transition: Housing, Markets and Public Policy*. Wiley Blackwell, Oxford, 2011; Crook, A. and Kemp, P. (eds) *Private Rental Housing: Comparative Perspectives*. Edward Elgar, Cheltenham, 2014.
32. Clapham et al., op. cit., p. 17.
33. See: Lowe, 2011, op. cit.
34. See: Dorling, 2014, op. cit., p. 160.
35. Collinson, P. The Guardian. at: http://www.theguardian.com/money/2016/jan/12/brighton-and-bristol-hit-hardest-as-rents-raised-by-an-average-of-18-in-2015.
36. Quoted in H.M. Government, 2017, op. cit., p. 11.
37. See: Pevalin, D., Taylor, M. and Todd, J. 'The Dynamics of Unhealthy Housing in the UK: A Panel Data Analysis,' *Housing Studies*, 23, 5, 2008, pp. 679–695.
38. Crook and Kemp, op. cit.
39. Reported in Anna Minton, 'Queezed out of the City,' The Guardian, 25 May, 2017.
40. See: Shelter. 'Complaints about landlords up almost 30 percent', Shelter, 2012. Accessed at: http://england.shelter.org.uk/news/previous_years/2012/october_2012/complaints_about_landlords_up_almost_30.
41. See: Tinson, A., Ayrton, C. Barker, K., Born, T. Aldridge, H. and Kenway, P. *Monitoring Poverty and Social Exclusion*. Joseph Rowntree Foundation, London, 2016.
42. Dorling, 2014, op. cit.
43. See: Bentley, R., Pevalin, D., Baker, E., Mason, K., Reeves, A. and Beer, A. 'Housing Affordability, Tenure and Mental Health in Australia and the United Kingdom: A Comparative Panel Analysis.' *Housing Studies*, 31, 2, 2016, pp. 208–222.
44. See: Clapham, D. *The Meaning of Housing: A Pathways Approach*. Policy Press, Bristol, 2005; Dupuis, A. and Thorns, D. 'Home, Home Ownership and the Search for Ontological Security,' *The Sociological Review*, 46, 1, 1998, pp. 24–47.
45. See: Howker and Malik, op. cit.
46. MORI, 2016.
47. English Housing Survey data quoted in H.M. Government, 2017, op. cit., p. 58, para 4.6.
48. See: Willetts, op. cit.
49. Ibid.
50. H.M. Government, 2017, op. cit., p. 10.
51. See the Nationwide figures on house price growth at: http://www.housepricecrash.co.uk/indices-nationwide-national-inflation.php

52. See: Andy Green. *Do We Need More of the 'Get Lost—Rich Twat'*
Spirit? LLAKES Blog, LLAKES Centre, UCL Institute of Education,
September, 2012. The figure is close to the £1.3 tn figure Martin Weale
calculated for the amount by which housing was overvalued, based on
its growth over and above the stock market norm of 5 percent pa. See
Howker and Malik, op. cit. p. 72.
53. Willetts, op. cit.
54. See: Shelter, 2012, op. cit.
55. See: Howker and Malik, op. cit.

CHAPTER FIVE

1. See: Appleyard, L. and Rowlinson, K. 'Home Ownership and the
Distribution of Personal Wealth: A Review of the Evidence.' Market
Trends Task Force. Joseph Rowntree Foundation, 2010, p. 14.
2. Ibid, p. 14.
3. Hills, J. et al., *An Anatomy of Economic Inequality in the UK*, Report
of the National Equality Panel, Government Equalities Office, London,
2010, p. 60.
4. Piketty, op. cit, Fig. 10.3, p. 344.
5. The Gini measure for personal wealth inequality derived from estate data will
differ from that for total in the Wealth and Assets survey since this measures
inequality in total household wealth. See Hills et al., 2010, op. cit., p. 60.
6. Bank of England. *Quarterly Bulletin 2007 Q1*, Volume 47 No. 1. See
also: commentary in Willetts, op. cit, p. 73.
7. See: Hills, J., 2010, op. cit.
8. Appleyard and Rowlinson, op. cit.
9. Ibid.
10. Hood, A. and Joyce, R. Briefing on 'Inheritances and Inequality across
and within Generations. Institute of Fiscal Studies, 5th January, 2017.
Accessed on 6.1.2017 at: https://www.ifs.org.uk/publications/8831.
11. See: Hills, 2015, op. cit.
12. See: Hutton, 2014, op. cit.
13. McCarthy, M., Sefton, J., Weale, M. *Generational Accounts for the United*
Kingdom. Discussion Paper, 377. National Institute of Economic and
Social Researh, London, 2011.

CHAPTER SIX

1. H. M. Government, *Building Our Industrial Strategy*. Green Paper.
January 2017.
2. See: Blanden and Machin, 2007, op. cit.

3. See: Green, 2013, op. cit.
4. Quoted in Ibid, p. 20.
5. See: Green, Green, and Pensiero, 2015 op. cit.
6. See: Green, A. 'Lifelong Learning, Equality and Social Cohesion,' *European Journal of Education*, 46, 2, May 2011, pp. 228–248.
7. See: OECD, *PISA 2009 Results. Overcoming Social Background: Equity in Learning Opportunities and Outcomes*, OECD, 2010b, Table 11.1.2, p.31.
8. See: Green, and Pensiero, 2016, op. cit.
9. Green, Green, and Pensiero, 2014, op. cit., Figures 7 and 8, p. 14.
10. Ibid, Figs. 17 and 18, p. 25.
11. See: Nickel, S. and Layard, R.. *Labour Market Institutions and Economic Performance*. Centre for Economic Performance, LSE, London, 1998; Bedard, K. and Ferrall, C. 'Wage and Test Score Dispersion: Some International Evidence.' *Economics of Education Review* 22, 2003, pp. 31–44.; Damme, D. 'How Closely is the Distribution of Skills Related to Countries' Overall Level of Social Inequality and Economic Prosperity?' *OECD Education Working Papers*, No. 105, OECD, Paris, 2014.
12. See: Wilkinson and Picket, 2009, op. cit.; Green et al., 2006, op. cit.; Green and Janmaat, 2011, op. cit.
13. Nicola Pensiero calculates that skills inequality in the non-migrant 16–65 population is negatively and quite strongly correlated with average levels of skills in the OECD Survey of Adult Skills data. The Pearson correlation coefficients are—0.64 in case of literacy and—0.78 in case of numeracy and are both significant at the 0.001 level. See: Green, Green, and Pensiero, 2015, op. cit. 2015, footnote 1.
14. See: Green, A. and Mostafa, T. *Pre-School Education and Care—a 'Win-Win' Policy?* LLAKES Research Paper 32, Institute of Education, London, 2011.
15. See: Heckman, J., 'Effects of Child-Care Programs on Women's Work Effort', *Journal of Political Economy*, 82, 1974, S136–S169.
16. See: Whitty, G. and Anders, J. *How did New Labour Narrow the Achievement and Participation Gap?* Research Paper 46, LLAKES, UCL Institute of Education; Lupton, R., and Obolenskaya, P. *Labour's Record on Education: Policy, Spending and Outcomes 1997–2010. Social Policy in a Cold Climate.* Working Paper No. WP03. London, 2013.
17. OECD. *PISA 2010b, op. cit.*, p. 31.
18. See: Hanushek, E. and Woessmann, L. 'Does Educational Tracking Affect Performance and Inequality? Differences-in-Differences Evidence across Countries.' *Economic Journal*, 116, 510, 2006, pp. C63–C76; Hanushek, E. and Woessmann, L. (2010). 'The Economics of International Differences in Educational Achievement.' NBER Working Paper 15949, National Bureau of Economic Research, Cambridge, M.A., 2010; OECD *PISA 2006: Science Competences for Tomorrow's World*, OECD, Paris, 2007.

19. Schütz, G., Urspung, H. and Wößmann, L.. 'Education Policy and Equality of Opportunity.' KYKLOS 61, 2, 2008, pp. 279–308. Van de Werfhorst, H. G. and Mifs, J. 'Achievement Inequality and the Institutional Structure of Systems: A Comparative Perspective,' *Annual Review of Sociology*, 36, 2010, pp. 407–428.

20. See: Van de Werfhorst et al., 2010, op.cit; Wößmann 2005, op. cit.

21. The OECD finds no relationship between levels of between-school competition and average system performance across countries (but a negative effect of educational equality). See: OECD, *PISA 2012 Results: What Makes Schools Successful? Resources, Policies and Practices*, Volume IV. OECD, Paris, 2013.

22. The OECD analysis of PISA 2012 data suggests that greater school autonomy over budgets has no significant effect on overall performance in maths. However, systems giving schools more autonomy in relation to course content and textbook choices tend to perform better. See OECD, 2013, Ibid.

23. See: Wiborg, S. 'Neo-liberalism and Universal State Education: the Cases of Denmark, Norway and Sweden 1980–2011'. In: *Comparative Education*, 49, 4, 2013, pp. 407–423.

24. See: Stephen, P., Jenkins, A, Micklewright, J. and Schnepf, S. 'Social Segregation in Secondary Schools: How does England Compare with Other Countries? *Oxford Review of Education*, 34, 1, 2008; Green, A. 'Le Modèle de l'École Unique, l'Égalité et la Chouette de Minerva', *Revue Française de Pédagogie*, 164, 2008, pp. 15–26.

25. OECD, 2010b. Table 11.5.1, p. 185.

26. OECD. *PISA 2006: Science Competences for Tomorrow's World*, Vol 1. OECD, Paris, 2007. p. 194.

27. See: Stephen et al. op cit.

28. See: Casey, L. *The Casey Review: A Review into Opportunity and Integration*, Her Majesty's Stationary Office, London, 2016. Accessed 12 Feb 2016 at: https://www.gov.uk/government/uploads/system/uploads/attachment_data/file/574565/The_Casey_Review.pdf.

29. See: Mortimore, P. *Education under Siege: Why there is a Better Alternative*. Policy Press, 2013; Green, A., 2008, op. cit.

30. See: Wilby, P. 'School Sixth Forms: an Outdated Luxury,' *The Guardian*, March 29, 2016. Accesed on 25 Nov 2016 at: https://www.theguardian.com/education/2016/mar/29/school-sixth-forms-outdated-colleges-comprehensive-education.

31. Sainsbury, D. *Report of the Independent Panel on Technical Education*, April 2016, p. 67.

32. Ibid, p. 41.

33. H.M. Government, 2017, op. cit.

34. Ibid, p. 36.
35. See: Green and Zhu, 2010, op. cit.
36. Wolf, A. *Remaking Tertiary Education: Can we Create a System that is Fair and Fit for Purpose?* Education Policy Institute, 2016, pp. 22–24.
37. For accounts of the key role of the polytechnics in Singapore's economic development see: Rodan, G. *The Political Economy of Singapore's Industrialisation.* London, Macmillan, 1989; Green, A, 2013, op. cit.; Brown, P. et al., 2001, op. cit.
38. See: Green, A. 2013, op. cit.
39. See: Crawford, C. Crawford, R. and Jin, W. *Estimating the Public Cost of Student Loans,* Institute for Fiscal Studies, 2014, p. 2.
40. Ibid, p. 26.
41. Browne, J. *Securing a Sustainable Future for Higher Education. An Independent Review of Higher Education Funding and Student Finance.* October, 2010. Dearing, J.R. *The Dearing Report. Higher Education in the Learning Society.* HMSO, 1997.
42. The data are taken from the 2016 UK Labour Force Survey. We exclude the 342,000 born in the UK outside England since the majority of these would have been educated in UK universities outside England. According to HESA SFA 242 data (Table 7) 61 percent of Welsh, 95 percent of Scottish and 68 percent of Northern Irish undergraduates attended universities in their home countries. This will result in a small under-estimation of the total revenue raised from the tax. My thanks to Geoff Mason for these calculations.
43. The estimate assumes average annual fees of £9,000 for full-time students and £4,500 for part-time students. The total costs comprise: 1) £ 8,862,120,000 in fees for full-time students (984,680 x £9,000); 2) £ 631,890 000 in fees for part-time students (140,420 x £4,500); 3) £1.5 bn for maintenance grants and 4) £839,198 160 for government teaching subsidies to universities for these students (1,115,955 x £752). The total teaching grant from HEFCE to English universities in 2014/15 was 1.4 bn, which averages at £752 per enrolled student. Data for 2015/6 from HESA First Statistical Release 242 Tables 1a. and N. English first degree part-time students numbers are not available from HESA's publicly available data and so are estimated here from the full-time number plus a number for part -time students derived from the part-time to full-time ratio for UK first degree students (14 percent).
44. According to HESA data, part-time students represent an additional 14 percent on top of the registrations for UK and other European full-time students. We estimate the costs of part-time students at 50 percent of the costs of full-time students.

45. In 2015 about half of all undergraduate students, whose parents earned less than £25,000, received maintenance grants of up to £3,387.

Chapter Seven

1. The Government White paper (2017, op. cit., p.6) says the consensus is that we need 225,000–275,000 pa. The 'State of the Nation 2013' report by Social Mobility Commission says 3 m. in 10 years.
2. H.M. Goverment, 2017, op. cit.
3. Department for Communities and Local Government data quoted by Hannah Richardson in: 'Affordable Home Building Drops to 24 Year Low,' *The Guardian*, 18 Nov 2016 at http://www.bbc.co.uk/news/education-38015368.
4. See: This is Money. Accessed on 26 May 2017 at: http://www.thisismoney.co.uk/money/mortgageshome/article-3184763/Young-homebuyers-st.html.
5. Wainwright, M. 'Out of the Box: Councils Try Innovative Projects to Provide Social Housing,' *The Guardian*, 10 Feb 2017.
6. See Nationwide data at: http://www.housepricecrash.co.uk/indices-nationwide-national-inflation.php
7. H.M. Revenue and Customs. *Annual UK Property Transactions Statistics*. Accessed on 19.11.2016 at: https://www.gov.uk/government/uploads/system/uploads/attachment_data/file/438425/2015_AUKPTS_circ.pdf.
8. See: Orton, M. *Struggling to Pay the Council Tax: A New Perspective on the Debate about Local Taxation*, Joseph Rowntree Foundation, London, 2006, p.11.
9. See: Pope, T. and Roantree, R. 'A Survey of the UK Tax system.' *IFS Briefing note BN09*, 2014.
10. See: H. M. Government, 2017, op. cit.
11. Orton, M. 2006, op. cit., p.11.

Chapter Eight

1. MORI, 2014. Accessed, 1.2.2017, at: http://www.ipsosglobaltrends.com/optimism-and-generations.html
2. Hutton, W., 2014, op. cit.
3. See H. M. Government. Green Paper: *Building Our Industrial Strategy*, January 2017, p17.
4. See: Streeck, op. cit.

5. Stiglitz, 2013, op. cit.
6. Hutton, 2014, *op. cit.*
7. Streeck, op. cit.
8. Glyn, 2007, op. cit.
9. Ibid.
10. Crouch, 2011, op. cit.
11. See: Arrighi, G. *Adam Smith in Beijing: Lineages of the Twenty-First Century.* Verso, London, 2007.
12. Streeck, op. cit. p.58
13. Green, A. *Education, Globalization and the Role of Comparative Research: A Professorial Lecture*, Institute of Education, London, 2002.
14. James, H. *The End of Globalisation.* Harvard University Press, Cambridge, MA, 2001.
15. Martin, H. P. and Schumann, H. (1996) *The Global Trap.* London: Zed Books.
16. Hutton, 2014, *op. cit.*
17. Berry, C. 'The Rise of Gerontocracy? Addressing the Intergenerational Democratic Deficit. The Intergenerational Foundation, London, 2012, available at: http://www.if.org.uk/wp-content/uploads/2012/04/IF_Democratic_Deficit_final.pdf
18. Ibid, p. 54.
19. Ibid, p.35.
20. Quoted in ibid, p.14.
21. Howker and Malik, op. cit.
22. Berry, op. cit., p. 37.
23. See: Willetts, op. cit.

REFERENCES

Allen, M., & Ainley, P. (2010). *Lost generation? New strategies for youth and education*. London: Continuum.

Allmendinger, J. (1989). Educational systems and labor market outcomes. *European Sociological Review, 5*(3), 231–250.

Appleyard, L., & Rowlinson, K. (2010). *Home ownership and the distribution of personal wealth: A review of the evidence*. York: Market Trends Task Force. Joseph Rowntree Foundation.

Armstrong, A. (2016). Commentary: UK housing market: Problems and policies. *National Institute Economic Review, 235*(1), F4–F8.

Arrighi, G. (2007). *Adam Smith in Beijing: Lineages of the twenty-first century*. London: Verso.

Atkinson, A. (2014). After Piketty? *British Journal of Sociology, 65*(4), 619–638.

Ballarino, G., Bernardi, F., Schadee, H., & Requena, M. (2009). Persistent inequalities? Expansion of education and class inequality in Italy and Spain. *European Sociological Review, 25*, 123–138.

Ballarino, G., Bratti, M., Filippin, A., Fiorio, C., Leonardi, M., & Scervini, F. (2014). Increasing educational inequalities? In W. Salverda, B. Nolan, D. Checchi, I. Marx, A. McKnight, I. Tóth, & H. van de Werfhorst (Eds.), *Changing inequalities in rich countries: Analytical and comparative perspectives*. Oxford: Oxford University Press.

Bedard, K., & Ferrall, C. (2003). Wage and test score dispersion: Some international evidence. *Economics of Education Review, 2*(2), 31–44.

Bell, D., & Blanchflower, D. (2011). *Young people and the great recession* (Discussion Paper No. 5674). Bonn: IZA.

© The Editor(s) (if applicable) and The Author(s) 2017
A. Green, *The Crisis for Young People*,
DOI 10.1007/978-3-319-58547-5

Bentley, R., Pevalin, D., Baker, E., Mason, K., Reeves, A., & Beer, A. (2016). Housing affordability, tenure and mental health in Australia and the United Kingdom: A comparative panel analysis. *Housing Studies, 31*(2), 208–222.

Berry, C. (2012). *The rising gerontocracy? Addressing the intergenerational deficit.* London: Intergenerational Foundation.

Blanden, J., & Machin, S. (2007). *Recent changes in intergenerational mobility in Britain.* London: Sutton Trust.

Blossfeld, H.-P., Klijzing, E., Mills, M., & Kurz, K. (2005). *Globalisation, uncertainty and youth in society.* London: Routledge.

Boudon, R. (1974). *Education, opportunity and social inequality.* London: Wiley.

Breen, R. (2005). Explaining cross-national variation in youth unemployment market and institutional factors. *European Sociological Review, 21*(2), 125–134.

Breen, R., Luijkx, R., Müller, W., & Pollak, R. (2009). Non-persistent inequality in educational attainment: Evidence from eight European countries. *American Journal of Sociology, 114*(5), 1475–1521.

Brown, A., Kirpal, S., & Rauner, F. (Eds.). (2007). *Identities at work.* Dordrecht: Springer.

Brown, P., Green, A., & Lauder, H. (2001). *High skills: Globalization, competitiveness and skills formation.* Oxford: Oxford University Press.

Brown, P., Lauder, H., & Ashton, D. (2011). *The global auction: The broken promises of education, jobs, and incomes.* New York: Oxford University Press.

Busemeyer, M. (2014). *Skills and inequality: Partisan politics and the political economy of education reforms in western welfare states.* Cambridge: Cambridge University Press.

Busemeyer, M., & Iversen, T. (2012). Collective skill systems, wage bargaining and labor market stratification. In M. Busemeyer & C. Trampusch (Eds.), *The political economy of collective skill formation.* Oxford: Oxford University Press.

Bynner, J., & Evans, K. (1994). Building on cultural traditions: Problems and solutions. In K. Evans & W. Heinz (Eds.), *Becoming adults in the 1990s.* London: Anglo-German Foundation.

Bynner, J., & Roberts, K. (Eds.). (1991). *Youth and work: Transition to employment in England and Germany.* London: Anglo-German Foundation.

Casey, L. (2016). *The Casey Review: A Review into Opportunity and Integration.* London: Her Majesty's Stationary Office.

CEDEFOP. (2008). *Initial vocational education and training (IVET) in Europe: Review.* Thessaloniki: European Centre for the Development of Vocational Training.

Chartered Institute of Professional Development (CIPD). (2015). *Overqualification and skills mismatch in the graduate labour market* (Policy Report). London: CIPD.

Clapham, D. (2005). *The meaning of housing: A pathways approach.* Bristol: Policy Press.

Collinson, P. (2014). But-to-let return of 16.3 percent dwarfs other investments. *The Guardian, 26,* 4.

Confederation of British Industry/Pearson. (2013). *Changing the pace: CBI employment and skills survey.* London: CBI.

Crawford, C., Crawford, R., & Jin, E. (2014). *Estimating the costs of student loans.* London: Institute for Fiscal Studies.

Crook, A., & Kemp, P. (2011). *Private landlords in transition: Housing, markets and public policy.* Oxford: Wiley Blackwell.

Crook, A., & Kemp, P. (Eds.). (2014). *Private rental housing: Comparative perspectives.* Cheltenham: Edward Elgar.

Crouch, C. (2011). *The strange non-death of neo-liberalism.* Cambridge: Polity Press.

Crouch, C. (2016). *The knowledge corrupters: Hidden consequences of the financial takeover of public life.* Cambridge: Polity Press.

Crouch, C., Finegold, D., & Sako, M. (1999). *Are skills the answer? The political economy of skill creation in advanced industrial countries.* New York: Oxford University Press.

Damme, D. (2014). *How closely is the distribution of skills related to countries' overall level of social inequality and economic prosperity?* (OECD Education Working Papers, No. 105). Paris: OECD.

Department for Business, Innovation and Skills (BIS). (2011). *Returns to intermediate and low level vocational qualifications—Adding to the existing evidence base* (BIS Research Paper 53). London: BIS.

Department of Business, Innovation and Skills (BIS). (2013). *The international survey of adult skills: Adult literacy, numeracy and problem-solving skills in England* (BIS Research Paper No. 139). London: BIS.

Department for Education (DFE). (2015). *Statistical first release: Participation in education, training and employment by 16–18 year-olds in England: End 2014.* London: DFE.

Department of Trade and Industry (DTI). (1998). *White paper: Our competitive future building the knowledge driven economy.* London: DTI.

Dorling, D. (2010). *Injustice: Why social inequality still persists.* Bristol: Policy Press.

Dorling, D. (2014a). *All that is solid.* London: Allen Lane.

Dorling, D. (2014b). *Inequality and the 1 percent.* London: Verso.

Dumas, A., Méhaut, P., & Olympio, N. (2013). From upper secondary to further education. In G.-J. Janmaat, M. Duru-Bellat, A. Green, & P. Méhaut (Eds.), *The dynamics and social outcomes of education systems.* Basingstoke: Palgrave.

Dupuis, A., & Thorns, D. (1998). Home, home ownership and the search for ontological security. *The Sociological Review, 46*(1), 24–47.

Esping-Andersen, G. (2005). Inequality of incomes and opportunities. In A. Giddens & P. Diamond (Eds.), *The new egalitarianism.* Cambridge: Polity Press.

Esping-Andersen, G. (2009). *The incomplete revolution.* Cambridge: Polity Press.

European Commission. (1995). *White paper: Teaching and learning—Towards the learning society.* Brussels: European Commission.

European Commission. (2016). *A memorandum on lifelong learning. European commission, Brussels, 2000.* Retrieved 10, June, from http://europa.eu.int/comm/education/life/memoen.pfd.

Evans, K., & Heinz, W. (Eds.). (1994). *Becoming adults in England and Germany.* London: Anglo-German Foundation.

Felstead, A., Gallie, D., & Green, F. (2015). *Unequal Britain at work.* Oxford: Oxford University Press.

Gardiner, L. (2016). *Stagnation generation: The case for renewing the intergenerational contract.* London: Resolution Foundation.

Glyn, A. (2007). *Capitalism unleashed: Finance, globalisation and welfare.* Oxford: Oxford University Press.

Gould, G. (2015). *Wasted: How misunderstanding young people threatens our future.* London: Abacus.

Green, A. (1990). *Education and state formation. The rise of education systems in England, Europe and the USA.* London: Macmillan.

Green, A. (2000). Lifelong learning and the learning society: Different European models of organization. In A. Hodgson (Ed.), *Policies, politics and the future of lifelong learning* (pp. 35–50). London: Kogan Page.

Green, A. (2002). *Education, globalization and the role of comparative research: A professorial lecture.* London: Institute of Education.

Green, A. (2003). The many faces of lifelong learning: Recent education policy trends in Europe. *Journal of Education Policy, 17*(6), 611–626.

Green, A. (2008). Le Modèle de l'École Unique, l'Égalité et la Chouette de Minerva. *Revue Française de Pédagogie, 164,* 15–26.

Green, A. (2013). *Education and state formation: Europe, East Asia and the USA.* Basingstoke: Palgrave. (Revised and Extended 2nd ed.).

Green, A., Green, F., & Pensiero, N. (2014). *Why are literacy and numeracy skills in England so unequal? Evidence from the OECD's survey of adult skills and other international surveys* (LLAKES Research Paper 47). London: UCL Institute of Education.

Green, A., Green, F., & Pensiero, N. (2015). Cross-country variation in adult skills inequality: Why are skill levels and opportunities so unequal in Anglophone countries? *Comparative Education Review, 59*(4), 595–618.

Green, A., & Janmaat, J.-G. (2011). *Regimes of social cohesion: Societies and the crisis of globalisation.* Basingstoke: Palgrave.

Green, A., & Mostafa, T. (2011). *Pre-school education and care—A 'win-win' policy?* (LLAKES Research Paper 32). London: Institute of Education.

Green, A., Mostafa, T., & Preston, J. (2010). *The Chimera of competitiveness: Varieties of capitalism and the economic crisis* (LLAKES Research Paper 8). London: UCL Institute of Education.

Green, A., & Pensiero, N. (2016). The effects of upper-secondary education and training systems on skills inequality. A Quasi-Cohort analysis using PISA 2000 and the OECD survey of adult skills. *British Education Research Journal,* *42*(5), 756–779.

Green, F., & Zhu, Y. (2010). Overqualification, job dissatisfaction, and increasing dispersion in the returns to graduate education. *Oxford Economic Papers,* *62*(4), 740–763.

Greenwood, C., Jenkins, A., & Vignoles, A. (2007). *The returns to qualifications in England: Updating the evidence base on Level 2 and Level 3 vocational qualifications.* London: London School of Economics.

Gregg, P., Machin, S., & Fernández-Salgado, M. (2014). The squeeze on real wages—And what it might take to end it. *National Institute of Economic Review,* *228*(1), R3–R16.

Hanushek, E., & Woessmann, L. (2006). Does educational tracking affect performance and inequality? Differences-in-differences evidence across countries. *Economic Journal,* *116*(510), C63–C76.

Hanushek, E., & Woessmann, L. (2010). *The economics of international differences in educational achievement* (Working Paper 15949). Cambridge, MA: National Bureau of Economic Research.

Harvey, D. (2008). The right to the city. *New Left Review, 53,* 23–40.

Heckman, J. (1974). Effects of child-care programs on women's work effort. *Journal of Political Economy, 82,* S136–S169.

Hills, J. (2015). *Good times, bad times. The welfare myth of them and US.* Bristol: Policy Press.

Hills, J., Brewer, M., Jenkins, S., Lister, R., Lupton, R., Machin, S., et al. (2010). *An anatomy of economic inequality in the UK* (Report of the National Equality Panel). London: Government Equalities Office.

H. M. Government. (2017, January). *Building our industrial strategy* (Green paper).

H. M. Government. (2017, February). *Fixing our broken housing Market* (white paper).

Hobsbawm, E. (1995). *Age of extremes. The short twentieth century, 1914–1991.* London: Abacus.

Hodgen, J., Pepper, D., Sturman, L., & Ruddock, G. (2010). *Is the UK an outlier? An international comparison of upper secondary mathematics education.* London: Nuffield Foundation.

Howker, E., & Malik, S. (2013). *Jilted generation. How Britain has bankrupted its youth.* London: Icon Books.

Hupkau, C., McNally, S., Ruiz-Valenzuela, J., & Ventura, G. (2016). *Post-compulsory education in England: Choices and implications* (Discussion Paper 001). London: Centre for Vocational Education Research, LSE.

Hutton, W. (2010). *Them and us: Changing Britain—Why we need a fairer society.* London: Little Brown.

Hutton, W. (2015). *How good we can be. Ending the mercenary society and building a great country.* London: Abacus.

Institute of Manpower Studies. (1984). *Competence and competition.* London: Manpower Services Commission.

Jackson, M. (Ed.). (2013). *Determined to succeed? Performance versus choice in educational attainment.* Stanford: Stanford University Press.

James, H. (2001). *The end of globalisation.* Cambridge, MA: Harvard University Press.

Jerrim, J., & Shure, N. (2016). *Achievement of 15-year-olds in England: PISA 2015 national report.* London: DFE.

Judt, T. (2010). *Ill Fares the Land.* Penguin Books.

Kemp, P. (2015). Private renting after the global financial crisis. *Housing Studies, 20*(4), 601–220.

Keating, A., Green, A., & Janmaat, J.G. (2015). Young Adults and Politics Today: Disengaged and Disaffected or Engaged and Enraged? *The latest findings from the Citizenship Education Longitudinal Study (CELS).* LLAKES Research Brief. UCL Institute of Education. Accessed on 27 May 2017 at: http://www.llakes.ac.uk/sites/llakes.ac.uk/files/LLAKES%20young%20 people%20and%20politics%20briefing%20paper.pdf.

Kingman, D., & Seager, A. (2014). *Squeezed youth: The intergenerational pay gap and the cost of living crisis.* London: Intergenerational Foundation.

Kurz, K., & Blossfeld, H. P. (Eds.). (2004). *Home ownership and social inequality in comparative perspective.* Stanford: Stanford University Press.

Liu, Y., Green, A., & Pensiero, N. (2016). Expansion of higher education and inequality of opportunities: A cross-national analysis. *Journal of Higher Education Policy and Management, 38*(3), 242–263.

Lowe, S. (2011). *The housing debate.* Bristol: Policy Press.

Lucas, S. (2001). Effectively maintained inequality: Education transitions, track mobility, and social background effects. *American Journal of Sociology, 106*(6), 1642–1690.

Lupton, R., & Obolenskaya, P. (2013). Labour's Record on Education: Policy, spending and outcomes 1997–2010. *Social Policy in a Cold Climate.* Working Paper No. WP03. London.

Marginson, S. (2015). Global stratification in higher education. In S. Slaughter & B. Taylor (Eds.), *Higher education, stratification and workforce development: Competitive advantage in Europe, the US and Canada.* Dordrecht: Springer.

Martin, H. P., & Schumann, H. (1996). *The global trap.* London: Zed Books.

McCarthy, M., Sefton, J., & Weale, M. (2011). *Generational accounts for the United Kingdom* (Discussion Paper. 377). London: National Institute of Economic and Social Research.

Meschi, E., & Scervini, F. (2012). *Expansion of schooling and educational inequality in Europe: Educational Kuznets curve revisited* (GINI Discussion Paper N. 61). Amsterdam: Amsterdam Institute for Advanced Labour Studies.

Milburn, A. (2012). *Fair access to professional careers. A progress report by the independent reviewer on social mobility and child poverty.* Retrieved October 11, 2016, from https://www.gov.uk/government/uploads/system/uploads/attachment_data/file/61090/IR_FairAccess_acc2.pdf.

Minton, A. (2017, 25 May). Queezed out of the City. *The Guardian.*

Mizen, P. (1990, September). *Young people's experience of the youth training scheme: A case study of recent state intervention in the youth labour market* (p. 23). Submitted for the degree of Ph.D. dissertation, Department of Sociology, University of Warwick.

Mortimore, P. (2013). *Education under siege: Why there is a better alternative.* Bristol: Policy Press.

Nickel, S., & Layard, R. (1998). *Labour market institutions and economic performance.* London: Centre for Economic Performance, LSE.

OECD. (1996). *Lifelong learning for all.* Paris: OECD.

OECD. (1999). *Classifying educational programmes: Manual for ISCED-97 implementation in OECD countries.* Paris: OECD.

OECD. (2000). *Literacy and the information age: Final report of the international literacy survey.* Paris: OECD.

OECD. (2010a). *Education at a glance.* Paris: OECD.

OECD. (2010b). *PISA 2009 results. Overcoming social background: Equity in learning opportunities and outcomes.* Paris: OECD.

OECD. (2013a). *Skills outlook 2013: First results from the survey of adult skill.* Paris: OECD.

OECD. (2013b). *Education at a glance.* Paris: OECD.

OECD. (2013c). *PISA 2012 results: What makes schools successful? Resources, policies and practices* (Vol. IV). Paris: OECD.

OECD. (2013d). *PISA 2012 results: Excellence through equity; giving every student the chance to succeed* (Vol. 11). Paris: OECD.

OECD. (2014). *Education at a glance.* Paris: OECD.

Orton, M. (2006). *Struggling to pay the council tax: A new perspective on the debate about local taxation.* London: Joseph Rowntree Foundation.

Osborne, H. (2016, 25 November). London Property now Costs 14 Times Average Wage. *The Guardian,* 37.

Pevalin, D., Taylor, M., & Todd, J. (2008). The dynamics of unhealthy housing in the UK: A panel data analysis. *Housing Studies, 23*(5), 679–695.

Piketty, T. (2014). *Capital in the twenty-first century.* Cambridge, MA: Belknap Press.

Pope, T., & Roantree, R. (2014). *A Survey of the UK Tax system.* IFS Briefing note BN09.

Putnam, R. (2015). *Our kids. The American dream in crisis.* New York: Simon Schuster.

Raffe, D., Brannen, K., Fairgrieve, J., & Martin, C. (2001). Participation, inclusiveness, academic drift and parity of esteem: A comparison of post-compulsory education and training in England, Wales, Scotland and Northern Ireland. *Oxford Review of Education, 27*(2), 173–203.

Raftery, A. E., & Hout, M. (1993). Maximally maintained inequality—Expansion, reform, and opportunity in Irish education, 1921–1975. *Sociology of Education, 66,* 41–62.

Reich, R. (1991). *The work of nations: A blueprint for the future.* London: Simon and Schuster.

Rodan, G. (1989). *The political economy of Singapore's industrialisation.* London: Macmillan.

Sainsbury, D. (2016, April). *Report of the independent panel on technical education.*

Schoon, I., & Bynner, J. (Eds.). (2017). *Young people and the great recession: Preparing for an uncertain future.* Cambridge: Cambridge University Press.

Schütz, G., Urspung, H., & Wößmann, L. (2008). Education policy and equality of opportunity. *KYKLOS, 61*(2), 279–308.

Shavit, Y., & Blossfeld, H.-P. (1993). *Persistent inequality: Changing educational attainment in thirteen countries.* Chicago: Chicago University Press.

Silver, J. (2013). *Coming up short: Working-class adulthood in an age of uncertainty.* Oxford: Oxford University Press.

Smets, K. (2015). Revisiting the political life-cycle model: Later maturation and turnout among young adults. *European Political Science Review, 8*(2), 1–25.

Social Mobility and Child Poverty Commission. (2013, October). *State of the nation 2013: Social mobility and child poverty in Great Britain.*

Standing, G. (2011). *The precariat: The dangerous new class.* London: Bloomsbury Academic.

Stephen, P., Jenkins, A., Micklewright, J., & Schnepf, S. (2008). Social segregation in secondary schools: How does England compare with other countries? *Oxford Review of Education, 34*(1), 21–37.

Stiglitz, J. (2010). *Freefall: Free markets and the sinking of the global economy.* London: Allen Lane.

Stiglitz, J. (2011). *The price of inequality.* New York: W. W. Norton & Company.

Streeck, W. (2016). *How Will Capitalism End?* New York: Verso.

Sullivan, A., Heath, A., & Rothon, C. (2011). Equalisation or inflation? Social class and gender differentials in England and Wales. *Oxford Review of Education, 37*(2), 215–240.

Sutton Trust. (2014). *Internship or indenture.* Research Brief. London: Sutton Trust.

Thomas, V., Wang, Y., & Fan, X. (2000). *Measuring education inequality: Gini coefficients of education* (World Bank Working Paper). Washington, DC: World Bank.

Thurow, L. (1996). *The future of capitalism*. London: Nicholas Brearley Publishing.

Tinson, A., Ayrton, C., Barker, K., Born, T., Aldridge, H., & Kenway, P. (2016). *Monitoring poverty and social exclusion*. London: Joseph Rowntree Foundation.

Van de Werfhorst, H. G., & Mifs, J. (2010). Achievement inequality and the institutional structure of systems: A comparative perspective. *Annual Review of Sociology, 36*, 407–428.

Wainwright, M. (2017, 10 February). Out of the Box: Councils Try Innovative Projects to Provide Social Housing. *The Guardian*.

Warren, T., & Lyonette, C. (2015). The quality of part-time work. In A. Felstead, D. Gallie, & F. Green (Eds.), *Unequal Britain at work*. Oxford: Oxford University Press.

Whitty, G., & Anders, J. 2014. *How did new labour narrow the achievement and participation gap?* (Research Paper 46). LLAKES, UCL Institute of Education.

Wiborg, S. (2013). Neo-liberalism and universal state education: The cases of Denmark, Norway and Sweden 1980–2011. *Comparative Education, 49*(4), 407–423.

Wilkinson, R., & Pickett, K. (2010). *The Spirit Level: Why Equality is better for everyone*. London: Bloomsbury Press.

Willetts, D. (2010). *The pinch: How the baby boomers took their children's future— And why they should give it back*. London: Atlantic Books.

Wolf, A. (2015). *Fixing a broken training system: The case for an apprenticeship levy*. London: Social Market Foundation.

Wolf, A. (2016). *Remaking tertiary education: Can we create a system that is fair and fit for purpose?* London: Education Policy Institute.

Index

© The Editor(s) (if applicable) and The Author(s) 2017
A. Green, *The Crisis for Young People*,
DOI 10.1007/978-3-319-58547-5

Printed by Printforce, the Netherlands